P9-CEZ-955

Fed up with fads?
Had it with how-to books?
Losing patience with pat solutions
that really don't solve your problems?
This is the book for you.

Here is practical, sensible
advice, based on the Bible
and on the scientific findings
of modern psychiatry and psychology,
that will help you solve those
everyday problems in a lasting way.

FAITH IS THE ANSWER

Fawcett Crest Books
by Norman Vincent Peale:

A GUIDE TO CONFIDENT LIVING

THE AMAZING RESULTS OF
    POSITIVE THINKING

THE ART OF REAL HAPPINESS

ENTHUSIASM MAKES THE DIFFERENCE

THE POWER OF POSITIVE THINKING

THE TOUGH-MINDED OPTIMIST

SIN, SEX, AND SELF-CONTROL

STAY ALIVE ALL YOUR LIFE

YOU CAN IF YOU THINK YOU CAN

THE POSITIVE PRINCIPLE TODAY

FAITH IS THE ANSWER

A Pastor and a Psychiatrist
Discuss Your Problems

Norman Vincent Peale, D.D.
and Smiley Blanton, M.D.

FAWCETT CREST • NEW YORK

A Fawcett Crest Book

Published by Ballantine Books

New and Revised Edition

Copyright © 1950 by Norman Vincent Peale and
Smiley Blanton

Copyright renewed © 1978 by Norman Vincent Peale and
Smiley Blanton

Original Edition Published in 1940

Copyright © 1940 by Norman Vincent Peale and
Smiley Blanton

All rights reserved. Published in the United States by Ballantine Books, a division of Random House, Inc., New York, and in Canada by Random House of Canada, Limited, Toronto, Canada.

ISBN 0-449-20308-5

This edition published by arrangement with Prentice-Hall

Manufactured in the United States of America

First Fawcett Crest Edition: June 1979
First Ballantine Books Edition: November 1982

10 9 8 7 6

Contents

Preface

IT SHOULD NO LONGER SURPRISE ANYONE THAT A MINISTER and a psychiatrist join forces in writing such a book as this, for in both spheres of activity the objective is essentially the same: the renewal of faith when faith has been lost—faith in oneself, faith in one's fellow man, and faith in God.

It is difficult for the pastor to have adequate psychiatric training and equally difficult for the psychiatrist to have the opportunity to study the problems of religion at first hand. In this treatment of the problem, therefore, the pastor contributes the solution which he believes religion has to offer, and the psychiatrist writes from what he feels to be the vantage point of psychiatry.

But this work is not directed primarily toward the cure of pathological cases; it is directed toward the old problem of keeping well people well. In this way, we believe religion and psychiatry can and will make an ever-increasing joint contribution in the coming years, because the function of each is to help normal people live more normal, happier, and more worthwhile lives.

As far as possible the use of technical terms has been avoided, nor was it thought either feasible or desirable to make an extensive analysis of the cases that are cited. They should be evaluated with this in mind. And it seemed best for each author to keep closely within his own province, to remain as closely as possible within his own field, while availing himself of the cooperation of the other.

The personal incidents are related by permission, and, where necessary, real identity has been concealed in accordance with the confidential character of both the pastoral and the medical relationships.

In reissuing this book, the writers have become increasingly conscious of the composite nature of such an undertaking. They are deeply indebted to many people, both in the building up of the contents and for criticism of the form throughout the book, as well as in the preparation of the manuscript for publication. This, therefore, is an expression of the authors' appreciation and thanks to all who have so generously contributed.

NORMAN VINCENT PEALE, D.D.

SMILEY BLANTON, M.D.

ONE:

The Power
of Faith

The Power of Faith

SMILEY BLANTON

IN A WORLD IN WHICH CRISIS SEEMS ALWAYS IMMINENT, the fact that love and faith can keep us whole sounds a clear call to men and women ready for despair. If there is a lack of faith in ourselves and in others and, ultimately, in God, then the time has come to take stock. For faith can mean fruition in the emotional as well as in the spiritual sense. Without it we are nothing.

Many normal men and women find themselves strangely unhappy in their personal lives. Something seems to block them at every turn in the search for contentment. And they are constantly conscious of an almost overwhelming anger and sense of frustration.

Fortunately it is never too late to take stock, never too late to comprehend the causes of our feelings and of our behavior. To paraphrase the philosopher Spinoza, it is useless to weep, it is useless to wax indignant. One must strive to understand!

We have come where we are through many years and by many paths, and we cannot retrace the path easily. But if we search our minds and hearts for self-instruction, we do see that the key not only to our present personalities but to our present difficulties as well as in our past experience. This is particularly true of our childhood experiences; of our early relationships with our parents. And an analysis of these infantile relationships helps us to correct the maladjustments and failures in our present-day lives.

If we are willing to accept the fact that our present attitude rests on a base of our past experiences, then it will become clear why it is difficult for a person who did not have an adequate relationship with his own parents in childhood to have a supreme faith in God, for the worship of God has always been a projection of the parent-child relationship.

Once upon a time, long ago, we all of us had this faith. What became of it? Why did we lose it? But most of all, how can we win it back?

A woman, whom we shall call Mrs. A., wrote Dr. Peale the following letter, a letter which presents a very common problem which both minister and psychiatrist have to meet.

"I am an average woman with the usual amount of ability and the usual amount of courage; but I am utterly discouraged now about myself.

"'I've listened to your radio talks and read your books, and I've read quite a bit of psychology here and there. I'm modern and I know that you are. I wish it were possible for you to tell me a few things.

"My husband says I need a psychiatrist; my friends say I need a minister. But what in the world can religion do for a person who is just in a state of confusion and discouragement? I haven't even any sins worth repenting, unless the lack of faith is one. It is just that I don't seem to be motivated. I do a great many things, but none of them gets me anywhere.

"Has religion anything to say to me? And, if not, then has psychiatry?"

We suggested that she come to our clinic at the Marble Collegiate Church in New York and talk to both Dr. Peale and myself. It seemed strange to her to suggest that she talk to both the minister and the psychiatrist. She herself thought that consulting one was the alternative to consulting the other. That was because she knew the function of the minister but did not realize that the function of the psychiatrist is as much preventive as curative, and that he deals with fears and anxieties, with depressions and worries that assail all of us, just as the minister does, but with a different approach. Nor did she realize that psychiatry deals to a great extent with the average person whose adjustment has become temporarily out of balance.

Why was this woman depressed and confused? It is a fundamental law of human behavior that all of man's acts are caused by something, and our first task was to help her to comprehend this. And, since it is agreed that knowing something about the functioning of the body makes for more healthful living, it must be insisted that it is no less useful to know something about the functioning of the emotions.

In order to find the cause of Mrs. A.'s difficulties, it was necessary for us to learn as much as we could, both about her childhood and her present environment. She talked freely, being sure of our sympathy, and this is the story that she told:

She was the youngest of four daughters, and she had early gained the impression that her family was bitterly disappointed, at her birth, that she was not a boy. They gave her the name of Elizabeth, but used the nickname "Bill" for her always. And, for instance, although she wanted to wear the pretty dresses that her sisters wore, her father insisted on her wearing overalls. He often regretted at length, in her hearing, that he had no son to carry on his name and business.

Her mother was an anxious sort of person who worried a great deal about her husband and her children. She felt that her husband must be catered to and pleased at all costs, and she would never stand back of this child in her defiant efforts to be like the other girls. As a result, Elizabeth's attitude toward both her mother and her father was one of great ambivalence, and she let it be seen that she both loved and hated them. To add fuel to the fire, they actually seemed to like this show of anger in her; they considered it "masculine." She felt deeply rejected by her father, and not very much more loved by her mother.

The psychiatrist does not assume that such a belief on the part of the patient is necessarily justified by the facts of the case but, whether it was justified or not, the girl did feel deeply rejected. Whether true or not, it was truth to her! Since the parents of this young woman lived not far from the clinic, it was possible to have an interview with them.

They were astonished to learn of the depth of her resentment. They brushed it aside a bit and insisted that "Bill was a sort of pet name. They were certain that they had insisted on the overalls only because she had such a lovely slim little body that showed so freely and gracefully in them. But it was admittedly true that they had wanted a boy, and that they had regretted very much that she had not been one and, even, that they were "sometimes indiscreet enough" to mention it in her presence.

Now that they are all grown they are certainly helpful and affectionate toward her, and toward her husband and her children, but they admit to being somewhat estranged by her present anger.

What apparently happened was that, on the basis of a certain amount of fact, she felt as though she had entirely failed to satisfy her parents and had been completely rejected by them. Her earliest ideas about her parents were distorted and intensified to such an extent that it still influenced her thinking and her feeling. And this is not unusual. One often finds adults who have been profoundly influenced throughout their entire lives by their childhood immaturity of judgment. Their more or less mistaken concept of their parents, and not the reality, has done the harm.

A feeling of dissatisfaction and insecurity has permeated all of Mrs. A.'s relationships, not only those with her parents. She was never able to make a happy adjustment to the three "feminine" sisters, nor, later, to her husband, nor even to her own children. She is entirely unable to believe that the love she so wants from others, and which she feels so ready to reciprocate, is probably hers for the taking.

As if this were not enough, she finds herself entirely at odds with religion. She is unable to achieve any satisfactory relationship with the Creator. The feeling of rejection which arose long before, in the parent-child relationship, now prevents her from believing even in the love of God.

It would not have been adequate to this woman's development for her to have had a satisfactory mother, even though her father had been less loving, or the reverse. In a world in which the relationship of the sexes to one another is of such importance, it is necessary to grow up in an environment developed by both sexes and to learn to adjust satisfactorily to both.

To understand men and women one must first understand the amoral, anti-social structure of the very young child. The very young child is naturally completely self-centered. It is interested exclusively in its own sensations, needs, and satisfactions. It may be said to live only for itself.

As it grows a little older in its attitudes a change gradually occurs. Some of its self-love is diverted as its vision widens. It begins to love not only itself, but also those objects outside itself which first contribute to its happiness. Its love includes the mother first, then the father.

At this early period a child's attachment to its parents is excessively strong. Even the shortest separation sometimes gives rise to great unhappiness on the part of the child, and thwarting of any sort seems often to develop grave apprehension. Nevertheless, it is necessary, in the exigencies of living, both to deprive and to thwart the child. It should be done with great care and insight. The child does have to be socialized. Eventually it does have to be made to conform to the needs of our civilization.

Examine the closeness of the relationship of the mother and father and child. The child is born from the mother's body and is usually fed by it. In its helplessness it is given constant and intimate care. The father-child relationship is not so intimate as the one between the child and the mother, but it is nonetheless equally important in the development of a good balance in the emotional life.

It is small wonder that perhaps the most appealing picture in the world is the "Madonna and Child," which portrays the ideal mother-child relationship. Nor is it surprising that, from the beginning, man has conceived of God as being a father; in the Christian faith, a loving Father. It could hardly be otherwise, since the idea of God is, to a great extent, derived from the early relationship with and the attitude toward the parents.

Slowly, as the child grows, there is developed in his mind an unfailingly powerful, unfailingly wise, and unfailingly benevolent image, a new figure watching over him, the figure of God. In this way the child's fundamental religious life is formed on the pattern of the parent. And the parent, object of this childish over-evaluation, should be most careful not to distort the child's concept of benevolence and justice, of fidelity and tenderness. The faith that has its foundation in love has no fear of itself; it is spontaneous and rewarding.

But this natural change of the child's adoration of his parents into a love of God is all too often interfered with by certain inhibitions which mar the love for the parent and so mar the love for the Creator. In another kind of parent-love relationship there is sometimes a parental love so overwhelming that the child, as it matures, becomes afraid of being dominated by anyone, either human or divine.

A week before John B. was born, his sister, the only other child in the family, was killed in a household accident. His mother lavished on him all of the love for the dead child as well as that part due him. Although she was in no way responsible for the accident, she had the guilty feeling that had she been foresighted enough it would not have happened. As a consequence, she tried to surround John with complete safety, and to foresee every eventuality.

He was not even permitted to enter the kitchen where the accident to his sister had occurred, and he was hardly permitted out of sight of the house until after he was twelve unless the mother or one of the maids was with him. Rough-and-tumble games were not allowed. The normal give-and-take between him and other boys was forbidden.

Although he was very much attached to his mother, he became very resentful of her domination and very fearful of her excessive affection. He felt, and rightly, that the love he was being smothered with was not in reality being given to him. He was acute enough to become jealous of the dead sister at a very early age. And he developed a whole system of suspicions toward all his mother's rules and regulations of his conduct.

As he grew older he became suspicious of the outside world as well. It was very difficult for him to make friends and practically impossible for him to keep them. In school, and later in his first jobs, he was resentful and uncooperative. He resented orders, even from those whose job it was to give them to him, and he frequently argued with his superiors, to the point of losing one position after another.

Inevitably, he broke with religion entirely and he surrounded the ethical concepts of Christianity with so many "ifs and buts" that they were practically negated, for the idea of being dominated even by God was intolerable to him.

This case, of course, was extreme. But it shows all the more clearly the process through which a child must go to have a healthy acceptance of social responsibility, and the way in which the ideas of and attitudes toward religion are formed by the human relationships.

It becomes obvious that the parent-child relationship requires a normal, adequate, and uninterrupted love; a love neither too great nor too small. Either too much or too little is a menace to the child's future love-life, and to his religious life as well.

The Greeks used the child's primary selfish stage of development to make one of their most beautiful legends—that of Narcissus, who saw his own reflection in a pool, fell in love with gazing at it, and was drowned. From this legend comes the use of the word "narcissism," meaning self-love. The child's greatest and earliest love is for himself, and from himself it flows to the parents. If the child's first love is inadequately returned, he draws back into himself and the result is narcissism.

Ann R. was an only child. Her mother was rich, beautiful, and socially prominent. Soon after Ann's birth she was turned over to nurses and governesses and she saw her mother for only the briefest period of each day. Her mother provided her with everything that money could possibly give her, but not part of herself.

As a result, Ann grew up aloof and unapproachable. Although outwardly gay and resourceful, she was really insecure and distrustful. At one period she suffered from profound depression, which, due to her excellent training in concealing what she felt, she was able to hide from everyone. She felt that no one could really be trusted, and, if anyone made overtures for her friendship, she very promptly began to look for the ulterior motive.

Her youth, charm, good education, and wealth were no satisfaction to her; even the very warmest interest that she could feel for people, or for anything outside herself, was pallid and negative.

Such a complete lack of interest inevitably includes a lack of faith in God, and although she had been a member of the correct congregation for her family and group, in late adolescence she drifted entirely away. Ann's case was an example of a narcissism in which the love she felt in her infancy, having been rejected by her mother, had turned back onto herself.

One cannot be always on guard against some "hidden enemy" and have any very satisfactory relationships. Such reservations are the death of love. If one feels that by submitting to love in any form he will be forced into some painful bondage, then love is impossible. And whether this feeling is based on fact or on fantasy, whether the injury to the psyche is from a real or an imaginary cause, it is a determining influence. It is only when the hidden inhibitions are removed that any real personal or religious relationship is possible.

Faith in one's parents as well as faith in God is based on love. One may, in his conscious mind, love with all his might, just as he may consciously do all in his power to realize an adequate relationship to God, but the efforts of the conscious mind are not sufficient; it is the unconscious mind that harbors the deepest feelings of our natures, and the deepest blockings of the free flow of our emotions as well.

It is only when we realize our limitations that we are able to receive help from outside ourselves. To some, help comes from philosophy or from ethics; to some, from religion. Life is too complex and unpredictable, too difficult and too severe, for us to face it with only our own feeble powers. Each of us feels the need for some sustaining power beyond and above himself, some embodiment of strength on which he may lean, or some resource on which he can draw.

The Power of Faith

NORMAN VINCENT PEALE

THE STEAMSHIP *Statendam,* ONE OF THE MOST BEAUTIFUL ships on the North Atlantic run, was bombed and burned at her dock in Rotterdam when the Nazis invaded Holland in World War II. Her skipper, my good friend Captain George Barendse, was on his way to America on another vessel at the time, his own ship having been temporarily removed from service because of war conditions.

When the Captain arrived in the United States he attempted to communicate with his wife and boy in Holland. He had read of the systematic bombing of Rotterdam, in which it was reported that a great many people were killed and a third of the city reduced to a shambles. All his efforts to reach his family were in vain.

His ship destroyed, his wife and child perhaps injured or even dead, his home city in ruins, his country overrun, the Captain came to my church that tragic Sunday morning in May, 1940. I saw him sitting in the pew seemingly crushed by this weight of sorrow. Partly for his sake I changed the selection of hymns, and the great congregation sang, as I have seldom heard, those noble hymns, "O God, our help in ages past, our hope for years to come," "A mighty fortress is our God, a bulwark never failing," and the stirring Dutch hymn, "We gather together." I was moved as I observed the sturdy Captain, one of the world's greatest seamen, singing with tears in his eyes of the indomitable faith in his heart.

Later the Captain lunched at our home, during which a great spiritual experience took place. He told of his experiences in Europe. We talked of his ship, which we all loved, and on which we had sailed, and of his family. The Captain, a man of profound faith, controlled but obviously suffering intense agony of spirit, and talking almost to himself as though alone, prayed a noble and courageous prayer when I asked him to say the blessing:

"God, help me not to hate; give your guidance in thought, in speech and in action to those who rule over the countries in war and . . . may your will be done and . . . your kingdom come." The words came one by one, slowly, as if hewn out of his soul. "God watch over my wife and boy. Before my wife was mine she belonged to you, Lord; before my little boy came to me he was yours, Father. They are in your hands. I trust you. May your will be done."

Again he searched his soul. "I pray for Hitler. God guide Hitler. He has great power over men's lives. You can change his heart, God. Help me not to hate Hitler. Help me to mean that, O God."

There at our table, at a simple family dinner, we sat awestruck before a great Christian. In this Dutch Captain, undaunted amid ruins, we saw the superb grandeur of the Christian faith; the magnificence of soul and spirit which it creates in human beings. Something caught at our throats and stirred our hearts as we watched the triumph; the ineffable victory of faith in the soul of a man. It would have been understood if there had flashed out hate, revenge, bitterness and inconsolable grief.

His prayer was said very quietly and simply as among

close and understanding friends, but it had an eloquence all its own that will never be forgotten. The Captain had a secret that stood him in good stead in those troubled times. His faith was strong enough to sustain him and enable him to see clearly and not be blinded. He had a faith by which he actually seemed to grip God's hand. He trusted God so completely that with supreme confidence he rested everything in God's hands, and so to him came peace and power.

A young woman in my church is the daughter of a prominent physician who at his death bequeathed her a substantial fortune. The property, however, was involved in litigation. The daughter had no funds to fight the suit, but a lawyer, an old family friend, came to her assistance, advancing the required funds and himself taking the case.

At the end of a long trial, to their great surprise, a verdict was returned against them. She had lost all she had expected to possess and the sum advanced by the lawyer friend was also gone. Together they walked from the courthouse and went slowly down the street. After they had walked silently for some distance, the lawyer turned to the young woman.

"Is anything wrong?" he said. "Aren't you feeling well?"

"Why yes, of course," she replied. "I feel perfectly well. Why do you ask?"

He looked at her in astonishment. "Don't you realize what has happened? You have lost everything and are penniless! Yet you are not panicky or hysterical; you give no sign of going to pieces nor are you even upset. Instead, you are so calm that I fear for you."

The young woman replied, "Come over into the park to that bench and I will explain to you."

They crossed into the park and she said, "You may not understand, but all through the trial I have prayed that God's will should be done. I could not pray for victory for myself unless God wanted it so, and I have prayed that the trial should result according to his will. The verdict is against me and while I do not understand it, somehow I know it is God's will and I accept it and feel only peace in my heart."

He looked at her in amazement, but saw only calmness and control written on her face. Her sincerity was impressive.

Months passed in which the young woman, who had expected ample resources, was compelled to struggle against adversity. But her sincere faith carried her through and she was able to support herself.

One night in a dream she had the strong impression she should take the case to a higher court. She told the lawyer of her feeling, which persuaded him to reopen the case. After some weeks a new verdict was handed down, this time in her favor. Moreover, she received by this verdict substantially greater benefit than would have been granted had she won the first action. She walked out of court with her trusted friend, who turned to her and said, "I have a new name for you. From now on you will be 'Little Miss Faith.' "

This incident emphasizes the importance of the young woman's wholehearted and sincere prayer that God's will be done. She wanted nothing for herself unless God willed it so and was content when the answer seemed to be adverse. Her desire and purpose was entirely spiritual. Her utter self-abnegation and completeness of personal surrender opened her nature to an unhindered flow of divine power. The incident is tinged with wonder and so may be disparaged by some who, living on a purely human basis, never expect wonders to happen. But a great Master once, when he saw that his disciples had no real belief in the possibility of "miracles" happening, marveled at their unbelief. It bewildered and amazed him that their faith was such a poor thing.

I have cited these two incidents to show that in two lives, different save in the one particular of sincere surrender to God's will, it was demonstrated that faith is the answer. The roll of such victorious people could be called indefinitely, but we turn to the important question arising directly from these experiences. How do you have faith like this?

Men have long been told to "have faith." What I propose to do in this chapter is to show *how* to have faith. My purpose is to help every person who may read this book to acquire spiritual skill, that he may develop a useful, effective, and satisfying life. I believe most people sincerely desire the benefits given by faith but their trouble is they do not know *how*. They are ignorant of the techniques of faith and hence are unable to practice it. The average man vaguely feels that religion has sources of power that are available to him, but he does not know any workable method for tapping this power.

If I were to tell you that everything troubling you, every weakness, every unhappiness can be eliminated; if I were to declare that everything about your life can be strong and effective, what would be your reaction? Probably it would be skeptical or at least wistful, doubtful that such marvelous results are possible. Some people have never had anything great happen to them, so they doubt that any great thing can happen. They suffer from what a great thinker once referred to as "the vast inertia of the soul."

But it is a fact that any person's life can be so completely changed that every crippling thing which interferes with his well-being can be eliminated or effectively controlled. This is no academic assertion but one that can be fully documented from the experiences of many people in whom the most amazing results have been obtained. These people learned the technique of faith and so tapped a curative element so potent that no malady of personality could resist its health-giving force. And, like many epoch-making processes, it operates simply.

The art of having faith may be developed through two suggestions, if they are faithfully followed: (1) the practice of simple but habitual prayer and devotional meditation; (2) the surrender of your life in an attitude of childlike trust to the will of God.

The late Henry Drummond was one of the superior intellects and scholars of his time. Beyond this, he was a spiritual genius, one of those rare characters who gain acute insight into spiritual laws. Drummond's secret was so simple that anyone can put it into practice. He stated his formula as follows: "Ten minutes spent in Christ's society every day, aye, two minutes, will make the whole day different." Multiply one day by every day and add the cumulative effect of habit and the changed mental outlook, and you will understand how this brief period faithfully observed can change everything, even your entire life.

Some men, strong, radiantly happy, live as Morley said of Gladstone, "as from some great depth of being." Examination of their daily program reveals regular periods of spiritual meditation. Drummond tells us that a few minutes daily spent in thinking about Christ and in consciously and sincerely seeking to secure His power will make the whole day different. This simple practice pro-

duces control over fears, weaknesses, and those tragic inep-
titudes which interfere so disastrously with success in life.

Wordsworth discovered the amazing values in a daily
period of spiritual meditation. His method was unusual
but rewarding, if we may judge by the quality of his mind
and character. It was his custom every day to meditate on
a few of Jesus' words, reading them slowly and endeavor-
ing to bring out their full meaning. He would say, "I wonder what Jesus meant when he said that. What was the
expression on his face, the tone of his voice?" This approach served to make Christ come near to Wordsworth
as a vital living character.

The hurry and rush of our lives is often advanced as a
reason why the daily period of personal prayer and meditation is impossible today. This, of course, is false. We
have ample time for what we *want* to do. It is possible for
every person to be alone for at least ten minutes every
day to relax body, mind, and soul, to open himself to God
and allow the divine energies to flood his receptive spirit.

There is a quality of the mind through which, with
practice, we can retire into ourselves and be in our own
quiet inner temple. On a train, or bus, or rushing subway
train, we may close our eyes, turn our minds to Christ
and withdraw from the busy world into a few minutes of
communion that will give us calm strength and imperturb-
able poise for the day.

I stress this practice, for it is a workable method for
developing faith. Live with Christ in daily spiritual association and your faith in God will become deep and certain.
It will make God a real factor rather than a vague concept.
An old blind Indian in the West, a magnificent person with
inner peace and kindly spirit, revealed the source of his
strength when he said, "It is easy to believe in God when

you live alone with him in the dark." He knew how to have faith because spiritually he lived with God.

I could write page after page of theory about how to have faith, but I will save you much reading by saying that if you will definitely set aside a few minutes, ten or even five, or as Drummond says, two minutes, to think about God and Christ, to confess your sins, to pray for those who have done wrong against you, and to ask for strength, and if you do this consistently day after day, a true faith will before long begin to send spiritual health and power through your personality.

A Chinese gentleman, a successful broker, recently told his story in our church clinic. It was a spiritual narrative, full of tragedy and rising to stirring drama. He came of a wealthy family and had every opportunity that wealth and social connections afford. He ultimately lost his wife through his dissipation and his money went the same way, the bulk of it through gambling. His health failed and a nervous breakdown made him unfit for any except very limited activity.

At this juncture he met some people whose joy and delight in life amazed him. It awakened the hope that there might be a way out of his sad failure. They told him the way was by faith, but the advice was futile. Faith was just the thing he did not have, either in God, his fellow man, or himself. But he was one of those rare souls who, once being convinced of great possibilities, is not daunted by any obstacle, however formidable.

He began a daily plan of communion with God, a wise friend having told him that this was the way to faith. Perseverance was difficult because of his nervous state and the dulled condition of his mind. But he kept at it desperately, feeling it was his last hope. For thirty minutes each morning he gave himself to a period of meditation and asked four questions:

1. What have I to thank God for during the last twenty-four hours?

2. What sins have I committed in the last twenty-four hours?

3. What does God want me to do?

4. Whom should I pray for?

The first two questions he limited to twenty-four hours because he felt the memory is inclined not to be specific unless the period of analysis is short.

As a result of this practice he overcame his disability. His mind began to function with its old-time efficiency. Today he is a happy man.

Sometimes in my interviews, when deep springs of experience have been opened, I have clearly felt the presence of Christ. It was so when this gentleman asserted his positive conviction that faith in God had remade his entire life, including his health and business.

The second and ultimate method for having faith is simply to *have faith*. Many people get lost exploring abstruse procedures, unaware that the secret is to believe by an act of trust. It was for this reason that Christ told us we could not enter his kingdom until we had a childlike heart.

The New Testament says, "According to your faith be it unto you." We receive good in direct proportion to the amount of faith we exercise. "Lord, I believe; help thou my unbelief," is the attitude that opens the door to new life. In plain words that means, "I trust you, O Lord. I believe, even though I cannot see how it can be. I believe even though shadowy questions haunt my mind." The spirit struggles to believe, triumphing over the weak doubtings of the earth-bound body. The release of power that comes with this victory of faith is the most impressive phenomenon of human experience.

I was asked to call on a patient in a tuberculosis hospital. This man said he had been helped by a radio program I was giving each week and wanted to talk with me. I went to see him at considerable expenditure of time, for the hospital was some distance from the city, but it proved to be very worth while—one of my most inspiring and enlightening experiences. I found this man on a mattress resting on a board because of the condition of his spine. His hand was off at the wrist, but he was one of the happiest men I ever met. I who had gone to comfort him was myself comforted, even thrilled by the story he told.

He was taken to the hospital and given up to die. He had been a successful lawyer, with a wife and two sons. Everything he owned went into the battle to save his life.

At the time he became hospitalized he was having frequent hemorrhages with severe pain. He was in an apparently hopeless condition. It was at this juncture that he listened to the radio talk in which occurred this quotation from the New Testament, "I can do all things through Christ which strengtheneth me."

"You said," he explained, "whoever you are, wherever you are, and in whatever condition or circumstance, if you surrender your life completely to God and put your trust in him you can obtain Divine power by which you can win over anything.

"You also spoke of the amount of faith that would help us. 'Even as a grain of mustard seed.' This seemed to me like a small investment for the return offered."

Looking straight at me, this man said, "I had heard that sort of thing all my life—that is, when I went to church, which was not too often—and it never moved me. In fact," he continued, "I guess I never really knew what it meant. But this time it came over me like a wave that it was true. I bowed my head and did just as you said. I guess I was at the end of my rope and I meant it absolutely when I put my life in God's hands. Then a strange thing happened. I felt a surge of peace. I came to have a conviction that regardless of the number and pain of hemorrhages nothing could ever hurt me again. I went farther, repeating my surrender every day, several times a day, and one day I came to believe that my hemorrhages would stop. They did stop and I've had none to this day." (This conversation took place two years after the spiritual experience which he described.)

With a happy smile, he continued: "I am slowly getting better, but that is not the chief thing that has happened to me. The main thing is this strange new strength, this wonderful inner peace, this absolute sense of being attached to the very power of God himself. We, my family and I, have had to face many difficult problems. Again and again we have been caught in what seemed a blind alley with no way out, but God opened a way every time and he always will."

Looking at that heroic and inspiring man, I knew I was listening to one of the most amazing yet authentic accounts of God's grace that has ever come to my attention. We both knew that day that we were talking about no imaginary happening but were awed by the real experience of a man who in his dire need stumbled upon the greatest thing that can happen to a human being—the actual release, through faith, of the power of God in human experience. There is in religious faith, available for our benefit, a greater power than we realize.

TWO:
The Hidden Energies of the Mind

The Hidden Energies
of the Mind

SMILEY BLANTON

NOTHING THAT HAPPENS TO US EITHER WAKING OR
sleeping is lost; all experience is stored in our minds.
Some of it is obviously in our conscious minds, in the part
of our memory that we are aware of. But by far the
greater amount of our memory material, although consciously forgotten, is really only repressed below the level
of conscious memory.

What evidence is there to support this theory? Long before the days of modern psychiatry or psychoanalysis, the
study of hypnotism showed clearly the existence of this
reservoir of memories. Dr. August Hoch, in his lectures to
students, told of an impressive demonstration in the office
of Dr. Morton Prince, one of the early workers in hypno-
sis. As an experiment, Dr. Prince put a woman patient
into a deep hypnotic sleep.

"Five minutes after you wake up," Dr. Prince said to
her, "walk to the mantelpiece, pick up a photograph there,
and ask me a question about it."

The woman awoke with no conscious memory of this
suggestion. She sat down next to Dr. Hoch, who started a
conversation with her. Dr. Prince meanwhile busied himself at his desk. Five minutes later, almost to the second,
the woman suddenly interrupted her conversation with

Dr. Hoch. She walked over to the mantelpiece and picked up the photograph, just as she had been told.

"Excuse me, Dr. Prince," she said, "isn't this some member of your family?"

"No," he replied. "Why do you ask?"

"Well, I've seen it here before," she explained, "and the picture seems to resemble you. I wondered if it were not some member of your family."

Actually, the photograph had been placed on the mantelpiece for the first time that very day.

Without the theory of the existence of the unconscious mind one cannot account for the ability to differentiate things during sleep. In a hospital some internes who were on call slept four in a room. An electric buzzer was used to summon them, with a different signal of long and short buzzes for each interne. The four soon got to the point where each would wake up at his own call but never hear any of the others.

But the unconscious mind is more than a storehouse of hidden memories. It also harbors what we felt about those events.

Nothing occurs to the individual from birth to death that does not have some sensation attached to it, either pleasurable or otherwise. With the memories that are repressed the attendant pleasant or unpleasant emotion is also repressed, until the unconscious mind becomes not only a vast storehouse of memory but of unreleased emotions also.

More than thirty years ago the psychologist William James described these repressed memories and emotions as "hidden energies." Modern psychiatry, after painstaking clinical observations, concludes that the source of this power is in the unconscious mind and that most of our actions are motivated by it.

It is true that most people go through life using only a very small part of this available energy. The rest constitutes a reservoir of idle power only waiting to be released into action.

But can it be tapped at will, can it be released for daily use? Can this stored hidden power be made to flow into use by intelligent understanding? Ordinarily, the releasing cause is some sudden, acute crisis. Then the submerged energies break through, to supply unexpected strength and endurance.

This surge of power is sometimes sufficient to transform the person's life. A striking instance was described to me by a Russian engineer living in Paris. The story concerned his mother, who had undergone harrowing experiences during the chaotic period of the Russian Revolution.

"My father, a former officer in the Czarist Army, had been shot dead before her very eyes by a roving band of revolutionaries. She herself had barely managed to escape from Russia with my brother and myself when we were ten and twelve years old respectively. Months of wandering ensued, amid terrible hardships that included long periods of semi-starvation. We finally reached Paris, where mother was able to establish a home for us.

"But the horrible experiences of the previous months had left their mark upon her. She developed diabetes and stomach ulcers, and began to have abdominal hemorrhages. Even more devastating was the emotional prostration which overcame her. She lost interest in everything and took to her bed, where, day after day, she lay like a living corpse. It was not an ordinary depression. It was as if the lifespring had been broken.

"Before she became bedridden my mother used to visit a nearby greengrocer's shop, run by a French peasant woman who had come to Paris after her husband and son had been killed in the war. Their mutual plight had created a bond of sympathy between the two women, and one day, after my mother had been ill for about six months, the shopkeeper came to call. I remember quite vividly what occurred.

"The French woman sat down at my mother's bedside and began talking quietly with her. I was washing dishes after the evening meal and at first paid little attention to the visitor's words, but finally a few phrases caught my ear and I stopped my work to listen. The peasant woman was trying to impress on my mother the necessity of recovering her health.

" 'You must not give up like this, dear friend,' she was saying. 'I know that you have suffered great sorrow and misfortune, but you still have the strength to be well again. You must think of your two children. They need you. It is your duty to live.'

"There was a moment's silence in the room before the peasant woman added, with great emphasis, 'It is the will of God.'

"There was complete quiet for several minutes. Then an extraordinary thing happened. My mother, though virtually bedridden for months, now suddenly rose to her feet. She put on the robe that lay on a chair by the bed, walked across the room to where I was standing and said quietly, 'I will wash the dishes, son.'

"I was so astonished I could hardly believe what I heard! I started to remonstrate, but mother brushed me aside.

" 'No, no," she insisted, 'I'll wash the dishes. You run out and play.'

"From that day on, my mother resumed her place in the family, quietly, courageously, and efficiently. Her physical ailments apparently disappeared. She improved rapidly, and for several years thereafter she remained practically a well woman."

The peasant woman's words, "It is the will of God," seemed to have come to the sick woman as a command from heaven. They supplied the impulse that released her reserves of energy and restored her to society.

Religious conversions too are often the result of influences which have slumbered in the unconscious mind for years. Many years ago in a Southern town there was a man who came of a very good family, but who operated several saloons and gambling houses. He was known as an "honest gambler," but his mode of life obviously ran counter to the teachings of his Christian mother. One day the great Southern evangelist, Sam Jones, preached a sermon against the evils of drink and gambling. The saloon proprietor was converted. The next day he closed up his saloons and poured the liquor into the gutters. He had decided to lead a new life, and he actually did so from that time on. The teachings "at his mother's knee" had never really lost their hold; had lain latent in his unconscious mind.

Sudden outbreaks of criminal tendencies may also arise in the same way. A man of upright character may startle the world by an unexpected crime, but he has not changed overnight. Anti-social impulses in his unconscious mind have gradually increased in force over a long period and have polarized at last.

Emotions in the unconscious mind are frequently powerful enough to produce severe bodily illnesses as well as mental ones. A young woman became sick as well as desperately frightened every time a thunderstorm occurred. Her own explanation was logical enough. These manifestations, she said, went back to an incident some years before, when lightning struck a tree near which she was standing. But investigation revealed a different reason.

Her difficulty really had not started until three years after the incident of the tree. The intense fear came for the first time on a certain spring day when her father was staying home from work. He was a husky man who never stayed at home unless he was quite ill, and the daughter had a feeling that something was seriously wrong. As she stood by the window looking out over the darkening countryside, a heavy cloud swept across the hills, and the thunder rolled. A great fear rose suddenly in her mind about her father. He did die soon afterward. The next time there was a thunderstorm she was seized with panic. The thunderstorm had become bound up with her father's death. Between the two there was some obscure connection of which she was entirely unconscious. Yet it was strong enough to affect her thinking, her feelings, and her physical health.

The existence of the unconscious mind is no longer seriously disputed. The question, "Do these hidden energies really exist?" has been answered. But establishing their existence would have no practical value unless it led to a way of probing the unconscious, investigating its structure, and developing a method to free its hidden energies and cure the conflicts and distortions which mar the daily work-life, play-life, and love-life. Fortunately for ailing humanity, there is an effective therapy. It owes its discovery and development to the remarkable work of the late Sigmund Freud. Freud produced a technique for helping solve these conflicts. Freud showed that dreams are usually disguised, distorted, symbolic fulfillments of childish desires. He showed a definite relation between dreams and the mental and emotional ills that suppress our powers, or derange them and thus cause psychic disorders. His scientific method of removing these repressions and unraveling these distortions still remains unimproved as a means of probing into unconscious processes.

Dream analysis shows that the unconscious contains a large store of infantile wishes, conflicts, and repressions. Most of these arise out of the child's relationship to his parents. The very young infant, as we know, is at first a helpless creature whose every need is met for him. His personality is composed of egocentric wants. But a conflict arises between his ego and the outside world which ends only with death.

The child obviously cannot have every wish satisfied, although his infant experiences have led him to expect this. Since it was once true, he has developed the fallacious belief that his mere wish should produce its own fulfillment. The wish and the act, to his mind, become one and the same thing; he tends to live as if the magic carpet were not a fairy tale but a fact. When his wishes are denied, he becomes enraged and frustrated. He wants to strike back at the reality which thwarts his desires. When he is made to do something that he does not like: when he is sent to bed or has had a dangerous toy taken away from him, or he is made to get out of the bathtub, he shouts or thinks, "I hate you! I hate you!" Normally, this hatred is not very strong, and it is assimilated as the child grows up. Yet the frustration persists, and to a very profound degree.

The child's strongest love relationship is with the mother and father, and he resists the necessity of giving up this cherished relationship. He tries to cling to his infantile love, to dominate his parents. His parents may fail in meeting this critical situation; they may not love him enough, or they may love him too much, or they may give him their love at too great a price.

The psychological weaning of the child may be prolonged or it may occur too suddenly. The child, feeling rejected because of this necessary weaning, reacts with a more or less strong antagonism. But for his own satisfaction he must retain the loving attention of his parents. His hostility, therefore, proves distressing to him and is repressed into his unconscious mind, where it continues to operate in a form no longer recognizable to him. Normally, the child does not altogether succeed in preventing this hostility from coming out. Characteristically, he loves his parents one moment, turns upon them angrily the next.

This ability of the infant to love and hate the same person almost at the same time is known as ambivalence. And the unconscious retains this contradictory quality all through life, influencing adult behavior in many unsuspected ways. A brilliant university student used to suffer agonies before he could decide upon the most trivial trip. He would start downtown, then stop and wonder whether he really ought or ought not to go. He would actually turn his body first toward and then away from his objective. This happened so much that he actually had to have his shoes reinforced with iron in order to keep from wearing them out by this turning.

Ambivalent impulses do not always reach such an obvious intensity. But many people have great difficulty in making up their minds about ordinary daily matters. They waste much energy going from one thing to another, and fixing on none. This ambivalent attitude is usually the result of unconscious childhood repressions. The ability to repress—to keep disturbing desires from coming into the conscious mind—is a necessary mechanism of mental life. It operates whenever impulses or wishes come into play that threaten the person's moral standards or bring him into painful conflict with his social group.

Yet these impulses, usually of infantile character, cannot be completely repressed. They may come out as dreams, or as ambivalent attitudes, or even as obsessive ideas and acts, just as old Doctor Johnson had irresistibly to touch all the lampposts that he passed.

Repression is also responsible for forgetting. When something unpleasant has been urgently impressed upon us, it evokes an antagonistic attitude in the unconscious and so influences the conscious mind that the act of forgetting takes place. Most people object violently to such an explanation. They refuse to believe that they might deliberately forget something they wish to remember. Their objection is based on the mistaken idea that every wish is what it appears to be—to be taken at its face value.

To understand the underlying ambivalence we must understand the impulses which are an important element of the unconscious, but to recall these so-called forgotten memories is often impossible without the aid of some such special technique as psychoanalysis. That which has made a really profound impression, which has been urgently impressed on the mind, is rarely forgotten; it is only deeply buried.

A certain young man suffered from profound suspicion and indifference. These feelings had developed during his early youth. His mother was an overconscientious woman who felt that she must not spoil her youngsters with too much affection, although she loved them dearly. The son, the youngest of her six children, had misinterpreted her attitude as a lack of love.

His psychoanalysis brought out a significant incident buried in his unconscious mind. One day when he was about six years old, his mother scolded him for committing some small misdeed. He got down on the floor and threw his arms around her knees.

"Mother," he cried passionately, "don't you love me? Won't you love me?"

She quietly pushed his hands away and walked off without saying a word.

"I felt," the young man told me, "as though the heavens had fallen." This culminating incident, forgotten for years, proved to have been the cause of his psychological difficulty.

Forgotten memories can retain their powerful hold in a peculiar way because the unconscious does not record the passing of events in the way the conscious mind does. Impulses repressed into the unconscious during infancy remain just as powerful after half a century as they were the day they were received. It may be said that the unconscious mind has not learned about the passage of time. This may not sound like common sense, but neither does it "make common sense" to say that water, a liquid, is composed of two invisible gases, hydrogen and oxygen, does it?

But the unconscious mind has other components than repressed wishes and forgotten unhappy memories. It is also the source of our most comforting feelings, of our loves and our strengths. Religion wells from the unconscious mind also. It was and it remains primarily an emotional experience; ordinary reason cannot be applied to it.

The unconscious mind also holds the tendencies of primitive man that have remained in all of us and that have been repressed into it. From it emerge superstitions such as the one about being thirteen at table, or about knocking on wood after bragging in order to insure the continuance of good fortune. The fallacy of "like-magic" comes from it also, as shown by such beliefs as the one that watering the yard will bring rain, or that eating red meat will make animals vicious.

People vary in the intensity with which they retain these tendencies. With some their entire lives are dominated by superstitions. But with all of us the remnants of primitive thinking have affected the modern way of thinking.

Indeed man's basic energy and strength depend on the instinct of self-preservation, or of reproduction, which permeates the unconscious. And although this basic energy and strength is, primarily, amoral and anti-social, it supplies the dynamic power of the individual. If it is not disciplined and made to serve useful ends, it will break through to distort the whole personality, or result in group distortions such as the aggression and cruelty at large in the world.

Yet man, by the use of reason, does have the ability to modify, change, and direct this primitive instinctive energy into useful channels. It cannot be suppressed, it must be controlled. The mechanism for such control is known as sublimation, a shifting of the energy from destructive goals to desirable ones.

The aggressive impulse of the young child, for instance, is in itself perfectly normal. It is a source of great energy. As such it needs proper direction. In ordinary life, the young boy's fighting impulse needs to be directed into such sports as boxing, or football, or mountain-climbing. So sublimated, it may later produce an explorer or a great engineer. Suppressed, it may lead to passivity, or effeminacy, or to overcompensated passivity which shows itself in pugnacity.

Side by side with the destructive impulses, it contains man's most constructive impulses. It is the source of his artistic imagination, of his finest creative capacities.

It is also the repository of man's conscience, of his sense of right or wrong. Part of this conscience exists in the conscious mind; but that part is relatively small. The real basis of man's morality lies in the deep unconscious mind. It is there that layer upon layer of early influences are laid down to form the foundation of his moral nature. Without this unconscious morality, life becomes extremely difficult. Situations do indeed arise in which careful deliberation by the conscious mind must precede any final decision, but ordinarily it is not feasible to stop every few minutes to think, "Is this right or wrong?" The person acts automatically. He feels "intuitively," as he himself explains, whether a contemplated deed is right or wrong. Thus, for instance, he relies on his early training to tell whether he should accept a bribe, perjure himself, or take advantage of his neighbor.

Man's problem is to use the energy of the unconscious mind in the most effective way. The infantile instincts must be sublimated to desirable ends. The primitive goals must be modified and the energy involved in them must be used for more mature purposes.

But this cannot be done by ignoring the less pleasant aspects of the unconscious mind. No ethical teaching, religious or secular, can produce good results unless it accepts man as he really is. Improvement will follow only when man recognizes the laws of his mind as laid down by his nature. He must understand that a large part of his unconscious is infantile and amoral, illogical and irrational, cruel and savage. He cannot afford to feel offended when told that he is often dominated by these motives hidden in the unconscious mind. If he rejects that fact, he will pay a penalty of illness and unhappiness. He must also appreciate that his deepest moral sense and his noblest aspirations exist side by side with anti-social forces. Then, through understanding and reason, he can bring order to the disordered forces of his mental life.

With man so "savagely surrounded, savagely descended," Robert Louis Stevenson eloquently said in his *Pulvis et Umbra*, "who should have blamed him had he been of a piece with his destiny and a being merely barbarous?" Yet we see men, instead, "still obscurely fighting the lost fight of virtue, still clinging, in the brothel or on the scaffold, to some rag of honor, the poor jewel of their souls! . . . They are condemned to some nobility."*

* *The Works of Robert Louis Stevenson*, Lothian Edition, Vol. VII, "Virginibus Puerisque: Pulvis et Umbra." Everleigh Nash & Grayson, London, 1881, p. 245 *et seq*.

The Hidden Energies of the Mind

NORMAN VINCENT PEALE

MEN HABITUALLY USE ONLY A SMALL PART OF THE powers which they possess and which they might use under appropriate circumstances." So said the eminent psychologist William James. Every person has it in him to be greater and accomplish more, according to this great expert in personality.

Deep within every normal individual is a vast reservoir of untapped power waiting to be used. In many, only a small trickle of power seeps to the surface, and on that we live and work. Little wonder that many are tired and unhappy, frustrated and ineffectual. A sixteen cylinder car, if it possessed feeling and reason, would not be very happy, or in any sense satisfactory, if it went sputtering and limping along on one cylinder. That is exactly what many are doing. This book is intended to help you learn and practice the secret of using your maximum power and ability.

The first step toward being what you *can* be is to know what you *are*. That is to say, no man can have the use of all his potential power until he learns to understand himself. The trouble with many people who fail in this life is that they go through the world thinking deep within them that they are ordinary, commonplace persons. Thus, having no fundamental belief in themselves, they dissipate their energies in unregulated living. Such persons live aimless and erratic lives very largely because they never had a glimpse of what life really can be and what they can become. Dr. Blanton has shown the possibilities for successful living which lie in the unconscious mind. How can religion help release these powers? The Bible, which contains, more than any book ever written, the most astute insight into and knowledge of human beings, tells the story of a young man who became satiated with life at the old home. Getting a sizable sum of money from his father, he went off and drank it up. We are told he went into "a far country," which is indeed an apt description. It is a far country, for some get so far into it they never get back. But this boy *did* get back. When his money was exhausted, his job lost, and he had gone the rounds of his associates getting only the cold shoulder, "he came to himself." The modern equivalent would likely be "he got wise to himself." Here is an example of the remarkable insight of the Bible. Here is a man who was ruining himself not because he was wicked, but because he was ignorant about himself. When "he came to himself," when he came to his senses, he experienced a self-discovery. He saw, as in a flash, that he had been on the wrong track; that he had been throwing his energies, his abilities, and his future away. "He came to himself" and saw with sharp discernment what he was and what he could become. Then he said to himself, "I will arise." From then on his life was an onward, upward movement. It becomes the story of aggressive, victorious living.

Christianity is coming to be more widely recognized every day as possessing the surest techniques for helping people realize themselves. It has an astounding genius for touching men's ordinary lives and unlocking doors behind which their personalities have long atrophied. Many people have the mistaken idea that religion restricts and imprisons. On the contrary, religion swings wide the door and invites men out to freer and happier lives. "He sets the prisoner free," says an old hymn, and that, of course, is why many ineffectual people are prisoners. Prisoners of the senses, prisoners of social customs, prisoners of themselves. Christ sets them free when, coming to themselves, they decide, "I will arise and go to my Father."

One result of the adventure of self-discovery is to become aware of our innate goodness. Whether you are prepared to admit it or not, you *are* a good person basically. No man can go far in low-level living without provoking the increasing protests of his finer self. It is impossible for any man long to escape the relentless challenge of the great personality within him.

Some years ago a play bore the title, *Six Characters in Search of an Author*. The play pictured a rehearsal at which several characters came bursting in, demanding to be played by the actors. This is an accurate picture of our lives. On our life's stage, great characters within us demand to perform in us before the world.

Nathaniel Hawthorne left among his papers an outline of a play, which he never wrote, but which intrigues us with its possibilities. It was to be a play in which the principal character never appears. Hawthorne with his superb genius could have made much of such an idea, but he did not need to write it for us, for you and I have played it often enough. It is tragic to think of a man on the stage of life playing only minor parts. He is the bigot, the coward, the defeated person, the liar, or the cheat. But for a man never to play the principal character within himself—that is tragical. Never to perceive and act the hero in his life; never to be the saint in him—that is a tragedy; never to have the principal character appear.

In every weak person there is a strong personality. In every evil person is a good personality. In every defeated person is a victorious personality. To become aware of this power within ourselves, is to practice the art of living.

This adventure of self-discovery also causes people to discover through their religious faith that in themselves there is a rugged character who cannot be discouraged nor defeated. Many modern people receive so many blows and hard knocks that the come-back spirit, the fighting spirit, has all but gone from them. Ready to admit they were defeated and that they could do nothing about it except complain and grow bitter, I have seen scores, even hundreds, of men and women turn to religious faith in an earnest attempt to get power into their lives. They put their lives, with all their problems, completely into God's hands, and God turns power into their lives like water into a reservoir long empty and dry. In the Bible we read, "But as many as received him, to them gave he power," and increasing numbers of modern people are discovering the truth of this.

A business man in his late thirties told me his experience. He was brought up in a devout home, but drifted from the religion of his college days. Later, he went into business, married and was swept along into a fast social crowd. His connection with spiritual values was exceedingly tenuous. Then hard times came. Business grew difficult. His domestic situation became complicated. His life and that of his wife were rooted only in material things, and such roots are insecure. To sum it up, life crashed in on him and his courage ran out. Life rained blow after blow upon him, and it was almost more than his insecurely buttressed spirit could take.

Then he encountered a radiant personality who possessed a depth of peace and confidence. This man was in a situation not unlike his own, but the similarity ended there, for this man was not beaten. On the contrary, he was overcoming adversity by an unwavering perseverance and sustained attack. My friend saw that this man was fed by what seemed an unfailing stream of power. He asked the secret and the answer was, "contact with God."

"But I have always believed in God," my friend said.

"Yes," the other man replied, "but have you ever absolutely and completely given yourself into his hands?"

My friend was forced to admit that he hadn't, but he did make this personal surrender, with the result that a spiritual transformation has stepped up his physical and mental energy.

He said an interesting thing to me recently.

"All my life," he declared, "I have been more or less 'around' religion, but it always seemed a rather dead and dull thing to me. Strange, how different it is now." And then he concluded, "But one thing is sure, when you actually take it into your life spiritually, it does everything it claims."

Dr. Blanton has pointed out how layer upon layer of childhood influences form in the unconscious mind the basis of our moral nature. Religion attempts to govern fundamental instincts and impulses by saturating the mind with spiritual ideals to such an extent that the automatic functioning of life will be on a basis of strength and goodness. Religion teaches us to allow only good and beautiful thoughts to enter the unconscious because of the obvious fact often demonstrated that the unconscious can only send back what was first sent down. Admit bad thoughts freely and bad motivation will be sent back. Habitually encourage thoughts of an elevated nature and the unconscious will inevitably return attitudes and actions of a corresponding quality.

As William James pointed out, the molecules and cells of our bodies and brains are storing up day by day every action, emotion, and thought, to be used either for or against us, quite automatically, in crises which ultimately arrive.

The Bible expresses the deepest possible insight into human nature in the phrase, "As he thinketh in his heart, so is he." That is one of the profoundest truths ever set down for man's guidance. The word "heart" is used to describe the innermost part of man's thought and feeling; what the modern psychiatrist refers to as "the unconscious." That is to say, a man is in the last analysis what he has been predominantly sending into his controlling thought center.

The ideas or thoughts which finally determine our actions and character are not those which we receive and examine in the conscious mind. It is not "as a man thinketh in his conscious mind" that constitutes his personality. That is only a reception office where thoughts, good, bad and innocuous, are examined and passed upon. Some are rejected. If these rejected thoughts are evil, their temporary presence in the conscious mind has done little if any harm. If they are good thoughts, they have had little opportunity to have any effect. But the thought, good or bad, which is passed upon favorably and received hospitably, becomes eventually the thought one "thinketh in his heart," and so presently it may be said, "So is he."

People come to us complaining of having what they

describe as "bad thoughts." These are thoughts of hate, or immorality, or dishonesty, or sometimes even murder. Such people are troubled by the feeling that the thought which passed through the mind has made them guilty of sin. They quote the Biblical passage, "Whosoever looketh on a woman to lust after her, hath committed adultery with her already in his heart."

Both Doctor Blanton and I in the church clinic have pointed out that no sin is committed merely because a thought enters the mind, provided it is not made welcome. Perhaps we may use the figure that the thought first passes into an anteroom, where it stands before the mind acting as a judge. No matter how sordid or evil, it has not touched the personality with its infamy nor in any way laid guilt upon the soul unless and until the mind acting as judge admits it with a welcome. If the mind decides against it and dismisses it, the personality is not only unsullied but is, on the contrary, by this act of rejection stimulated and strengthened in moral power. You cannot prevent the birds from flying over your head, but you can keep them from building nests in your hair.

A thought that enters the mind, is weighed and rejected, and is passed, condemned from the mind, leaves no stain of guilt but instead greatly increases spiritual power.

There can be no doubt that Jesus held this point of view, for in the passage quoted above, the phrase "looketh on a woman to lust after her" does not imply a passing and unadmitted impure thought but a definitely entertained desire. The word "lust," which is the important word in the passage, means a premeditated and active attitude implying an idea welcomed and pleasurably entertained.

In my experience as a pastor, I have known many

people whose lives were made exceedingly unhappy by their failure to make this important distinction between an evil thought examined and rejected, and an evil thought accepted and entertained.

Consideration of this problem, which affects many people, makes it plain that a conscious mind, morally discriminating and vigorous, standing guard over the unconscious mind, is profoundly essential equipment for happy and effective living.

That which is received and accepted by the conscious mind determines ultimately the automatic reaction of the unconscious and in effect may be summed up as character. Before every deed there is a thought or more properly a succession of thoughts. Before the thief steals with his hand he steals with his mind. Before the immoral act is performed the mind has already committed the offense. If the thought of a wrong act has never been favorably entertained by the mind, the act itself will never take place. The issue is determined, not at the moment of crisis by rational and objective thinking, but by the resistance or lack of it in the unconscious, a resistance which has been strengthened or weakened each time the conscious mind rejected or accepted thought.

In a small town one family had operated the local bank for three generations. Grandfather, father, and son in succession had filled the important position of banker to the community. The family was held in the highest esteem and respect. The great depression came, and the son, who had become president of the bank and had succumbed to the speculation mania sweeping the country, had overtaxed his ability to meet his obligations. He had to have money.

One night, alone in the bank, the thought of falsifying

the books came to him, but he resolutely put it aside. It returned again and again. No one would ever know. He could make good out of his earnings before the bank examiners would discover the default. The pressure became great. In other relationships, as it later appeared, he had played fast and loose with fidelity. His inner supports had been weakened.

The unconscious could only return what he had given it, and one night the hand crept out hesitantly but surely to perform the deed which sent him to the penitentiary and broke the long and honored tradition of a fine family. "As he thinketh in his heart, so is he." What we are will eventually appear. The mask will some day slip from the face. The truth will out.

In the unconscious are all the forces which make for our success or failure, our misery or our happiness. These forces, according to their strength, control the mind, determining our choices and decisions. In the unconscious lie hidden energies which can defeat us if not understood and properly used but which wisely used can endow us with great power. Religion says that when these hidden energies are brought under the influence of Christ as Master of life, the most amazing results appear in people whose lives were hitherto commonplace or defeated.

By the phrase "coming under the influence of Christ" we mean the acceptance of Christ's way of life as our own. Further than that, it requires an attitude which we call spiritual experience. The standard word for it is "conversion." It is a surrender of self to God by an act of faith, a wholehearted readiness to follow God's will.

This spiritual experience drives deeply into the personality, laying a controlling hand upon the unconscious mind, the inner life force, holding firmly in check the destructive elements, and releasing the hidden energies to produce a person of wisdom and power.

An outstanding Negro singer, Roland Hayes, writes of one of his experiences: "It was at one of my scheduled concerts in Berlin in 1924 that I had a terrifying experience. The French were occupying the Rhine and were policing it with Negro troops, and German indignation was running high. I was in Prague. The American Consul there received several letters protesting against my singing in Berlin, asking if an American Negro was to insult the spirit of Goethe, Schiller, and other great writers of Germany by singing plantation songs from cotton fields of America in Beethoven Hall. The Consul advised me not to go to Berlin. However, I went. On the night of my concert, I took a closed taxicab with my Negro accompanist to Beethoven Hall.

"The hall was packed with people, with hundreds standing. At eight o'clock I walked on the stage with my accompanist, to be greeted by a barrage of hisses full of hatred.

"I had never had that experience before. But I remembered my mission. I did then what I have always done at the beginning of a concert. It is my habit when I step on any stage to recall to myself that I am merely an instrument through which my mission is being fulfilled. I stood there with hands clasped before me, praying; praying that Roland Hayes might be entirely blotted out of the picture; that the people sitting there might feel only the spirit of God flowing through melody and rhythm; that racial and national prejudices might be forgotten.

"Usually when I do that sincerely the audience instinctively feels what is happening as I commune with my Father. But that was the hardest audience I ever faced. However, as I stood there I had no doubts. I stepped to the curve of the piano and stood there with my head up and my eyes closed letting the Spirit do its work and waiting for that hissing to die down. Two minutes, three, four, five, on into an interminable ten minutes, the hissing continued. I waited for silence. Would it ever come? Ten minutes passed, and the hissing and stamping of feet stopped abruptly.

"I spoke to my accompanist without turning my head from the audience and asked him to take from his music case Schubert's 'Thou Art My Peace.' It begins softly in almost a whisper. As the clear notes of the song floated out over the crowd, a silence fell on them. It was not a personal victory. It was the victory of a Power which is greater than I am, and it subdued the hatred in the audience."*

* William L. Stidger, *The Human Side of Greatness*, Harper & Brothers, New York.

THREE:
Fear, Worry, and Anxiety

Fear, Worry, and Anxiety

SMILEY BLANTON

FROM THE EASE WITH WHICH FEARS ARE BUILT UP, it would be easy to believe that they have some organic basis. It is more exact to say that they are drawn from some reservoir inside the mind. Actually, only two fears are believed to be present at birth: the fear of falling and the fear of loud noises.

It is very often asserted that fear is destructive. Yet this is not entirely true; when fear is felt about things that truly threaten security, it is protective. It is very fortunate that man has an almost unlimited capacity for learning fears; otherwise, he would have been eliminated long ago. A reasonable fear of lurking danger enables us to take a reasonable precaution against it. It is when it is incorrectly directed that it is destructive. Then it is as though a big-game hunter, upon hearing a sound, emptied his gun at random. Then, disarmed, he would find danger leaping upon him.

But our civilization and our method of rearing children have evoked morbid anxiety states in us all. Anxiety is chronic fear. The patterns of fear laid down in our infancy have dominated out whole emotional life.

We should indeed have fear of the amoral, cruel impulses which dwell in the deep levels of the unconscious mind, side by side with our impulses of love and generos-

58

ity. But these impulses and their effect on our behavior must be understood. Then the energy of the undesirable fear impulse which goes out in destructiveness can be redirected in the service both of the individual and of society. Misdirected fears may cause disorders of the emotional life so destructive that the victim is incapacitated.

But fear is fear, whether it is misdirected or not. One often hears it said: "She has nothing to fear. It is all imaginary." This is always a misstatement. All fears are real—none is imaginary. But the object of the fear is often imaginary, and the true cause of the fear must always be sought. If the cause cannot be found in the objective world, perhaps it may be found in the unconscious depths of the mind, where a record of all experience is kept, fresh and with undiminished energy.

Perhaps an example of how misdirected fear may disrupt our everyday life will help to clarify this point.

A young woman, Miss X., sought counsel from a minister for a distressing anxiety over the behavior of her brother, who was divorced but planned to marry again. Their church did not forbid the marriage of divorced people. Nevertheless, she felt that her brother's soul would be lost if he made this marriage. The minister, apparently turning from the immediate problem, said, "Tell me about yourself."

"Oh," she said, "I have had a very pleasant life. My father was about the most wonderful man I have ever known. My brother is too. I've had a few casual friends among men but I've never met a man who could compare with either my father or my brother!

"My childhood life was very happy. I went through college and now have a very lovely position with a man who is the head of a large firm. He entrusts me with a great deal of responsibility and I'm very happy in my work. I have the most wonderful boss in the world, too." Her face glowed with joy.

"My dear Miss X.," the minister said, "would you be greatly offended if I made a very personal guess about you? My only reason is to help you." "Oh no," she said, "say whatever you think will help me."

Then he said: "I believe that you are in love with your employer, and I believe the question of his divorcing his wife has at least been mentioned between you. Isn't that true?"

After tears and confusion, she admitted it to be so but said, passionately, "I'll never be responsible for breaking up a home. I know my employer's wife. She is a lovely woman. They have two lovely children. I'll never do that."

"That's fine," said the minister. "As long as you face the matter frankly, I'm sure something can be done about it. Now, do you see that your anxiety about your brother's behavior is in reality an anxiety about your own?"

It was clear from the story that she had a very strong overattachment for her father. This is not at all unusual. In the splendid book *The Happy Family*, by the late Dr. John Levy and Dr. Ruth Monroe, they tell the following story about their own little girl. Their daughter is talking and says:

" 'Daddy, when I grow up I'm going to be a plain lady like mother.'

"Thus did my handsome four-year-old daughter reject my proposal that she train for the Follies chorus.

" 'I'm going to have five little children,' she continued.

" 'That's lovely,' I replied appreciatively. 'And who is going to be the father of your babies?'

" 'Why, you, Daddy.' "*

This desire of the little girl to remain always beloved by her father is a phase that all normal children pass through, but for some reason, to return to the case of the distressed Miss X., the bond was so close that it was not loosened at the normal age, and she remained, in her unconscious mind, attached so deeply to her father that she could not arrive at any normal love relationships with men when she grew up. She had a pattern in her unconscious mind which compelled her to fall in love with a man who had a position of authority, and, preferably, one who had two children, as her father had. This unhappy pattern caused her to become attached to her employer, and even to discuss the possibility of marrying him should he divorce his wife. Further, she read into this very unethical person the character and ethics of her very moral father.

Since she was incapable of consciously facing the real cause of her anxiety, her unconscious mind found it necessary to invent a cause unconsciously, and to transfer her feeling of anxiety from herself to her brother. She was not really worried over the fact that her divorced brother planned to marry again: she was worried because she herself was tempted to marry her employer, who represented her father.

Morbid anxiety may thus be caused by unconscious motives, and anxiety which may transfer itself to some object other than the real cause. That she should be bound very strongly to her father is, of course, perfectly

* Dr. John Levy and Dr. Ruth Monroe, *The Happy Family*, Alfred A. Knopf, New York, 1938.

natural and right. Only when she permits her attachment to her father to dominate her adult life is harm done.

In this young woman the anxiety seems to be due to a conflict between her desires and her conscience.

The "still small voice of conscience" is not born with the human being. It is trained into him both consciously and unconsciously by the adults in the child's environment. It is developed both by what the child is told and by what he sees that others believe; by precept and by example, as we say.

Training the young human being to conform to the demands of human society is a delicate process. He must be taught the use of privacy for some of the purely physical functions. In eating, for instance, which in our civilization is a highly social function, he must be taught what we call manners. The Tuaregs, of North Africa, are said to think it shameful to eat in the presence of one another. In Mohammedan countries it is still generally considered to be a gross indelicacy for a woman to show her face in public. Their tabus seem strange to us: some of ours seem strange to other peoples. But to the young child all of them seem unreasonable. He must learn very delicate distinctions between what is permitted and what is not done. Very few children, indeed, go through this training without developing a sense of shame about the functions themselves.

Unwise or overzealous training can load the young child with a feeling of guilt in no wise justified by the occasion. He may in turn hand on to his children a greatly overcharged emphasis on the suppression of all sorts of otherwise innocent behavior. As a child grows older he is often able to correct these extremes of feeling. He finds that what he learned in his period of training to think so shameful was really not so. But very often in spite of this intellectual correction *the sense of guilt remains,* and the anxiety engendered by this sense of guilt attaches itself in an unreasonable manner to desirable behavior and thus wreaks havoc in adult life. The child's home education is informal, but it is nonetheless education. Since it so profoundly influences the entire adult life, it should be considered not only a part of education but the most important part.

In the child's education one of the most important tasks is teaching the nature of procreation and a correct attitude toward these facts. A wise parent not only explains adult mating at the most suitable moment but also maintains an attitude toward it that influences the child wisely. The mystery of mating and birth should not be involved in the child's mind with blushing, embarrassed parents. Such an attitude springs from false modesty and produces a sense of mistrust in the child's mind. Too often, this feeling eventually turns to one of disgust.

A child's desire to understand mating and birth is wholesome. The child who does not get this information from his parents or teachers will look for it elsewhere, or, worse still, repress his questioning of the whole problem as painful and perverse.

It should be apparent even to the most casual observer that if this curiosity of the child, springing so naturally to his consciousness, is suppressed at the time, giving him a feeling of guilt and anxiety about it, then harm is in the making. Such suppression has been known to affect an individual's entire mental and emotional life, with more or less disastrous results.

Curiosity, in a child, is a very valuable tool. Great care

must be taken to guide but not to suppress it. This is especially true of curiosity about procreation.

There are many cases on record in which children have failed in their schoolwork because of the suppression of their early curiosity in this direction. This writer once made a study in Minneapolis of brilliant high-school students who were failing in their schoolwork, and found that in more than half of the cases, their expression of this natural and healthy curiosity about life had been blocked in early childhood.

It is when old morbid anxieties attach themselves to these objective fears that such troubles ensue.

To return to the adult. Real fears rarely cause serious disturbances: poverty, war, ill health, loss of a loved person, rarely of themselves cause a collapse of his ability to adjust. He, like the apostle Paul, having done what he can, stands fast. He becomes adjusted even to the most dangerous occupations, or he leaves them. He either reduces and assimilates anxiety engendered by them to the point where it no longer bothers him or else he removes the anxiety by quitting.

In some circumstances, such as battle, for example, the strain of the actual situation, no matter how great, is borne by some with only the normal fatigue. Others who carry an overload of anxiety into the situation may find it intolerable, and, since physical escape is impossible, suffer a nervous breakdown. There may be no less bravery in the latter than in the former. The initial overload of anxiety with which each went into battle determines the capacity for adjustment. Most mental disturbances are a means of escape from morbid anxiety, from pressure caused by the fear in the unconscious mind.

We deceive ourselves, however, if we say that subjective fears are baseless. All worries, anxieties, or fears have a basis either in the conscious or the unconscious mind. In a sense, they can never be "cast off"; they must always be assimilated and worked through.

The line of demarcation between a reality fear and an unconscious fear is often very easy to see in another person, but hard to see in ourselves. Our own fears all seem reasonable! And this is very clever of the unconscious mind. The unconscious mind's main function often appears to be to misguide us and supply us with the wrong ideas. In that way it protects us from realizing how primitive, cruel, foolish, amoral, and often savage our own deep unconscious levels may be, and protects us against the painful self-knowledge necessary to remove these traits. Explaining away is so much more comfortable at the time. But not in the long run!

A man of seventy-five was in a state of extreme distress about his estate. He could think of nothing else. His investments, amounting to several hundred thousand dollars, were all in safe, gilt-edged bonds. He had tied his real estate to himself with the most cautious legal arrangements. His house, dappled by the sun through his handsome trees, could not possibly be lost to him. Yet he was worrying himself into infirmity over the fear that inflation, or a capital levy, or even a revolution would wipe out his fortune.

"Why are you so afraid?" he was asked.

"I'm afraid I will be left poverty-stricken in my old age."

That most of his old age was already gone he seemed not at all to realize. Nor would it have been possible to make him see that what he actually feared was death, although that was implicit in all his arguments.

Another case is that of a middle-aged woman who was compelled to care for her eighty-year-old father. The old man was cantankerous, demanding and domineering. Although quite wealthy, he refused to hire a nurse, insisting that this daughter care for him. Paid nurses made him nervous, he said. He refused to consider the obvious fact that he was making it impossible for his daughter to have any life of her own.

But his attitude was nothing really new in her life. He had always dominated her. Not only had he kept her from having any social life of her own, but he had also been the cause of her broken engagement to a young man whom she loved.

This woman was burdened with a strong anxiety state about her father. She would become panic-stricken when away from home and would hurry back to make sure he was not dead. Finally, her anxiety grew so great that she found it impossible to leave the house for any length of time. No deep psychological insight is necessary to grasp the cause of her anxiety: the primitive impulses of hate and antagonism that she felt for her father in her unconscious mind and which she ruthlessly repressed with her conscious mind.

Obviously, it is impossible to persuade such people out of such anxiety states. Their anxieties are real, and talk, especially deprecating talk, cannot help them out of their difficulty. Often their attitude is not only not rejected but instead is accepted as very worthy and noble. A feeling of vanity about how "selfless" they are—the clever unconscious mind!—protects them from a knowledge of the futility of their own behavior.

But an understanding of these unconscious desires, these instinctive urges that lie hidden from us in the recesses of our unconscious minds, can modify them. With knowledge and self-understanding the sick reactions can be rejected and replaced.

Every person suffering from excessive anxiety must first of all accept the fact that the anxiety will disappear only when he faces it on an adult level, a level of reality. But to do this we must know ourselves: we must become able to understand the secret impulses that spring from the unconscious mind.

Fear, Worry, and Anxiety

NORMAN VINCENT PEALE

IT WAS A STORMY NIGHT LONG YEARS AGO. THE BOY awoke suddenly from a terrifying dream. Where was he? A gust of wind rattled the window on which the rain coursed down in meandering rivulets. A crash of thunder followed, rolling and reverberating down the sky. Wildly waving branches made grotesque shadows across the windowpane.

"Mother," he cried out in fear. He sprang from bed; there was a flash of white feet across the carpeted floor and he was beside his mother's bed.

"Mother," he sobbed. A soft hand was on his head. Tender arms were about him.

"What are you afraid of, my boy? Do not be afraid; Mother is here—there is nothing to be afraid of." Presently she led him back to his bed, tucked him in, kissed him good night once more, and soon he was asleep again, this time soundly.

The boy, now a man, awoke in the night from a restless and troubled sleep. He had many worries. He lay staring into the dark. Hurriedly his agitated mind ran over his fears, and then over and over them again. Shadows—vague sinister uncertainties—rose out of the night. The same terror he had known as a boy was upon him. He wanted to call out for help, only now he could not turn to his mother. But he knew someone to whom he could turn. A verse from the Bible ran through his mind: "As one whom his mother comforteth, so will I comfort you."

So in the darkness the man said: "Father, what can I do? Help me." Then out of the night—or was it out of the depths of his soul (what matter?)—spoke a voice, and it said words he had heard long before from beloved lips: "What are you afraid of, my son? I am here. There is nothing to be afraid of." And so there came to his mind a great comfort.

Who was the boy—who was the man? Perhaps it was you, perhaps I. The story can probably be duplicated, in some part at least, in the life of every person today. But here is a great secret. Why did the boy receive courage from his mother? The answer is that he loved her and trusted her. He had absolute faith in her tender and protecting care. "Perfect love," you see, "casteth out fear." Why was the man given courage so that he was no longer afraid? Again the answer is that he loved God and trusted him. He had absolute faith in his tender and protecting care. Again, "perfect love casteth out fear." That is what real religion can and does do for people.

Religion requires a simple childlike trust in the goodness of God, and in his watchful care. It requires that we say in the words of the beautiful Twenty-third Psalm: "I will fear no evil: for thou are with me; thy rod and thy staff they comfort me." We begin to get somewhere with the art of living if we turn from our fears and look up to God and hear him say, as our parents said when we were children: "What are you afraid of? There is nothing to be afraid of, my child."

There are many men in America today who are failing or not getting ahead, and this is so because the free functioning of their intellectual and emotional capacities is inhibited by anxiety and fear. Here, for example, is a man who goes down to his office in the morning and sits down to a desk full of business.

This man needs to be able to draw fully upon his mental equipment to dispose effectively of the problems before him. But he is haunted by anxiety and fear. He is worried about the condition of the stock market, about meeting the pay roll, or about holding his job. He worries about the European situation or the condition of this country. He worries about his family, or how to meet the payments on his home. He worries about whether he has heart trouble or high blood pressure, or fears that some sin he committed will catch up with him and put its bony and terrifying finger into his business to his undoing. His powers should be drawn to a focus as the divergent rays of the sun are caught by the glass and brought to a point of heat. But his powers are drawn off in a score of different directions by the wide sprouting of his anxieties, and the emotional and mental energy which he needs for success is lacking. Deeply buried anxiety in the unconscious mind is the cause of an astoundingly large number of inefficient careers in our time.

"What is courage?" a small boy recently asked his mother, and then added, "Is it like our cat when he arches his back and spits when he is afraid?"

His mother tried to think of a way to make the real meaning of courage clear to her son, for she believed, as Dr. Blanton says, that "the first and finest lesson that parents can teach little children is courage." She took him for a long walk in the country, and they finally came to a place where a destructive forest fire had raged. In a blackened, fire-swept field they saw one little red flower.

Pointing to that little, courageous, optimistic red flower, she said, "There is courage, my son—a fragile red flower growing in a fire-swept land." It is a good symbol of courage. Soon or late, the fires of adversity will roar across the life of each of us, and in the blackened desolation that remains it will be hard to see any hope, but in that hour we must project the flower of courage in a fire-swept land. That one flower of courage will be the forerunner of restored life.

What is the cure for anxiety and fear? How many have this kind of courage? The best answer to that question is not any comment of mine or suggestion from the experts, but a statement found in the Bible. It reads, "Take no thought for your life, what ye shall eat, or what ye shall drink; nor yet for your body, what ye shall put on . . . But seek ye first the kingdom of God, and his righteousness; and all these things shall be added unto you."

What does that mean? It means that we are not to worry about the necessities of life, but to strive for inner peace and mental, emotional, and spiritual harmony, developing an organized and integrated personality which will help us to meet life so effectively that these necessary things will indeed "be added unto you." This admonition from the Bible implies what is directly stated in many other Scripture references—that an habitual resting of our worries upon the goodness of God through faith releases power into our lives. Through this power we accomplish what would otherwise be impossible.

One practical way of putting into practice this wise advice is to develop the habit of not talking about our anxieties and our worries. The average anxious person is constantly telling everybody how worried and apprehensive he is about everything. It should be recalled that speech has greater effect on emotion than thinking has. An actor, for example, can talk himself into the desired emotions he wishes to portray. Get your anxiety out of your general conversation and it will tend to drop out of your mind. On the other hand, it is advisable to go to someone who has the insight and skill to help you become free from your worries.

Go to your minister, or your priest, or your rabbi, or your psychiatrist and unburden yourself. Tell everything that is on your heart, including your sins, real and imaginary, the haunting sense of guilt, and every suppressed desire. This confession, this unburdening of yourself, will throw sunlight into every dark corner of the mind, drive out the shadows, bring blessed relief, and open the way for complete healing of the malady of anxiety.

Religion is a practical method for solving this problem. Many people do not understand present-day religious practice; they think of it as something quite removed from everyday life. Thereby they miss the one thing that could make them happy and successful and useful. Some time ago I was in a police station—a voluntary visit—and in talking with a burly sergeant I told him I had just given a radio talk on "How Religion Can Conquer Nervousness." He was astounded and said: "I never heard of religion having anything to do with nervousness. I thought religion was just going to church and acting as decent as you can."

"Go read your Bible," I replied, "and you will find that religion is a medicine for every human ill."

"I sure will," he said, "because if religion can do what you said, I'll have to try a little."

It will do everything it claims to do for the man who really tries it.

How does the fact that we turn to God in trust and faith relieve us of our fears? For one thing, when a man gets his mind on God, he gets it off himself. Fears accompany excessive thinking about oneself. They are nurtured by the ego-centered attitude as a nest is warmed by a sitting hen. Our minds sit on the nest of our real and imaginary fears, mostly the latter, and soon we have hatched a flock of new little fears, and they grow up rapidly. We need to engage in more physical activity and less introspection if we are to eliminate fear from our lives.

Physicians tell us that abstract thought, in which fear is generated, comes from the higher brain centers, while physical activity, such as walking, comes from the lower brain centers. Surgeons have developed an operation in which portions of the frontal lobe of the brain, or higher thought center, have been removed in an effort to literally cut away worry and fear. It is reported that with the removal of a portion of the higher brain in certain carefully selected cases, fear actually disappeared. I know nothing of the scientific and practical value of such operations, but it would be splendid if we could go to a doctor and, as we have our tonsils removed, have those sections of our brain eliminated which produce destructive fear and worry. Still, many people would have fewer fears if they would use their feet more in walking and their brains less in introspection—if they would give themselves to some worthwhile physical activity.

Mary Ellen Chase says: "Manual labor to my father was not only good and decent for its own sake, but, as he was given to saying, 'it straightened out one's thoughts'—a contention which I have since proved on many occasions: indeed, the best antidote I know to a confused head or to tangled emotions is to work with one's hands. To scrub a floor has alleviated many a broken heart, and to wash and iron one's clothes has brought order and clarity to many a perplexed and anxious mind."*

For this reason a well-known psychologist wisely advised a young man to run around the block every night until he was dead tired, as an effective means toward conquering his fears.

But there are other and better things to do in conquering fear than to run around the block. Some of us could not run around the block if we tried. We tip the scales too high, or there is a bad heart or high blood-pressure—and, of course, what would the neighbors think? If you ran around the block in New York, the policeman would probably take after you on the suspicion you had robbed a bank.

The one *sure* method of eradicating fear from the mind is by surrendering one's life to God. By that I mean, not attempting to pluck fear out by a process of effort and struggle or by power of will. This only serves to implant it more firmly in the consciousness. The surrender of life to God means that all fear and worry is laid before Him and the future is left in His hands in perfect trust. We are then able to avoid any worried thought for the morrow, for God knows our needs and will take care of us.

For my part, I have found it absolutely true that when I sincerely put my life in God's hands and trust Him to take care of me, He does so with amazing kindliness. This is one of the greatest secrets in the world. It gives peace and strength beyond calculation. Let all your fears go— give them to God. He will not let you down. Did you ever

* Mary Ellen Chase, *The Goodly Fellowship*, The Macmillan Co., New York.

carry a tired child in your arms? You will recall the complete relaxation of the little body. The child rests in your arms entirely free from tension. There is in him no fear that he will be dropped. Feeling this trust, you hold the little form all the closer and with greater care, for you cannot fail such complete confidence.

If this kind of love and faith passes between grownups and tired, sleepy children, how much more profoundly does God take to his heart adults who are tired and worn in the dark nights of this life?

A stout heart and a courageous spirit constitute a basic necessity for this life. Samuel Johnson understood this fact when he said that courage is the primary virtue! "Unless a man have that virtue, he has no security for preserving any other."

I once spoke to the students of a New England university, and afterward went home to dinner with an old and wise professor. As we sat by the fire that stormy day, he presented me with a little book by J. M. Barrie, saying: "You will need this often. Make a companion of it."

He was right. It was Barrie's famous essay on "Courage," and I have always kept it nearby. Its deep philosophy, written in his inimitable style, has meant much to me when my courage has ebbed. In it, among other things, Barrie says: "Pray for courage with your daily bread, for courage will keep you light-hearted and gay and you *must keep* light-hearted and gay."

How to have courage is a practical problem faced by every reader of this volume.

One of the most pathetic things in life is to see human beings struggling against great odds, trying desperately to muster courage. It is also inspiring, for it reveals the magnificent heroism of the average man. The more we watch people fighting gallantly against discouragement and hardship and pain and fear, the more wonderful we feel they are. The great need of this life is to develop courage.

Many people miss the best rewards of life simply because of their inability to develop courage.

Browsing through an old library recently, I came across a book written by a very wise man of a bygone generation. The book told a story showing that ebbing courage has been a problem in every generation.

The book told of a man who had acquired a claim in a far western gold field. The claim was in a lonely spot in the mountains. When the man started to dig for gold, he found evidence that much work had been done on the claim a long while before. Far into the excavation he found an old rusted pick, its handle rotted off but its point sticking firmly in the rocky soil. He went to work and, to his amazement, just a few feet beyond where he had found the pick he came upon a rich vein of gold. He felt there was some tragedy connected with the old pick and later he heard the story.

A prospector years before had learned of the probability of a rich strike in this locality, had staked out his claim and had gone to work. Day after day, until his back ached unbearably, he worked with his pick, but never a glimpse of gold did he see. Gradually the acid of discouragement crept through his system, eating away his resolution. His courage slowly ebbed, and one day in desperation, and with a sense of complete futility, he drove his pick hard into the rocky earth, gathered up his belongings, and went away. The passing years rusted the pick and ate away the handle.

The tragedy of ebbing courage which failed just short of success was not revealed until many years later, when the prospector of our story came and found, a few feet farther on, the vein which would have fallen to the first man, had he been able to solve the problem of failing courage. He is fortunate indeed who, no matter how desperate his condition, how unpromising his prospects, still has growing within his soul the red flower of courage.

What is the secret of this kind of courage? When courage fails, the secret is to fill your mind and saturate your consciousness with simple and trusting faith in God. I emphasize this procedure, for it is the solution to the problem of fear.

There is a quotation from the Bible which every man with ebbing courage would do well to hang on his bedroom wall, where he could look at it every morning before starting out to face the day's struggle, and every evening, that it might leaven his unconscious mind as he slept. That great sentence is this: "In all these things we are more than conquerors through Him that loved us."

I do not mean to say that every person who belongs to the church, or who believes academically in God, has the kind of faith that keeps courage from ebbing, but I do say that every individual I have ever known who truly practiced the faith of the New Testament always kept a sturdy heart. I have never yet known a man to be defeated who believes in and practices—and the emphasis is on practices—sincere faith in God. I can produce scores of present-day people, young and old, from every walk of life, who in their own experience discovered that they could become more than conquerors "through Him that loved us."

Trust endows one with the much-to-be-desired ability to face problems relaxed, rather than tense. Relaxation of the personality is really an evidence of faith and trust.

When you lie down at night, you trust your bed. You believe it will support you. You do not lie rigidly in your bed, fearing that at any moment it may collapse with you on the floor. If you did, you would not get much sleep. Knowing your bed to be trustworthy, you yield your body to it in complete muscular relaxation, and presently you fall asleep.

The man who believes absolutely in God, in the Divine reliability and goodness, does not hold himself mentally and spiritually rigid, fearful that any moment something is going to happen to him, but on the contrary, rests in complete confidence that all things work together for good to them who believe in God. As a result, he has peace in his mind and quietness at the center of his life. He becomes neither panicky nor discouraged, for he knows that God watches over him.

This relaxed and peaceful state of mind gives him a clear brain, and makes possible the free exercise of all his faculties. Thus he is able to attack his problems with every ounce of ability he possesses.

The relaxed man is the powerful man. The rigid, tied-up personality is defeated before the battle starts. Many people break under life because of this rigidity. They have no capacity for the give-and-take of circumstance. They do not have in their souls the element that gives buoyancy and flexibility with which to ride out the storms of life.

Once I was on a large ocean liner in a fairly rough sea. I was on the bridge deck with the Captain. At that point on the highest deck above the water, the rolling of the ship is accentuated, and when the vessel keeled over it seemed to me each time that it was in danger of going so far that it would be utterly unable to right itself. I actually found myself pressing my feet against the slanting deck in an instinctive attempt to help bring the ship back to a normal position, to the amusement of the Captain. Each time, when it seemed that the ship would surely be unable to recover, she came back as gracefully as a bird, and, like a thing alive, sailed steadily ahead.

I asked the Captain to explain this flexibility of his ship, and the principle she depended on to keep from being hurled over on her side and sunk. He said: "You are undoubtedly familiar with those toys that have a curved base with a weight inside. Those toys cannot be knocked over because, even if struck vigorously, they instantly recover to an upright position owing to the shape of their base and their weight. An ocean liner is built on the same principle, having a curved base and being filled below her bottom deck with tanks containing thousands of gallons of fuel oil and of water. This simple principle keeps the ship upright."

If we fill our souls with the grace of God, we take aboard the ship of our lives that element which, when the storms come, not only will keep us afloat, but will enable us with grace and spiritual flexibility to ride victoriously through the tempests of fear and anxiety.

FOUR:
Conscience and the Sense of Guilt

Conscience and the Sense of Guilt

Smiley Blanton

ANXIETY IN ITS SIMPLEST FORM IS NORMAL IN BOTH MAN and animal, and is a device for adjustment to others of the same group as well as for control inside the group. Anxiety may be in part defined as a mild chronic form of fear.

The child has a natural tendency to criticize his own behavior, a tendency which is gradually enlarged by the critical attitude of his parents toward him and his habits. He knows early in life that he ought to do certain things that are "right," and not do other things that are "wrong."

This self-critical tendency is enhanced, during the growth away from childhood, by a sense of guilt or self-reproach over too strong a desire to retain the childlike relationship to the parents beyond childhood. A primitive Australian savage and the civilized American have this in common; in the break which must come to all in the infant-parent relationship, unconscious guilt becomes resentment, or antagonism, or sometimes hate. Children of three and four often say to their parents when they feel their relationship threatened by discipline: "I hate you!" "Go away!" "I wish you were dead!" This is an outward manifestation of an inward anxiety, and unless these impulses are carefully handled by the parent, they may be repressed into the unconscious to distort the entire adult life. Clear-cut examples of what occurs in a lesser degree in "normal" people can often be seen in the acute emotional illnesses.

Miss Elsie A. felt as a child that her mother neglected her. The mother, overworked, was often tired and irritable. She did love her little daughter but failed to bring any imagination to a difficult situation. Elsie's father, on the other hand, paid her much attention. He carried her about on his shoulders, walked with her in the woods, took her hunting and fishing. As a result of both parents' attitudes she became strongly overattached to her father. She had few companions of her own age, and did not make friends easily at school. As a compensation, she worked hard at her lessons and did well in her classes, finally graduating from high school with honors.

She took some technical training and after several years obtained a fine position. She was twenty-five when she took the position, and she held it for twenty-five years. She transferred to her employer the loving, adoring attitude she had held toward her father; there was, however, never anything but the most formal relationship between the two. In her position she served so well that she became indispensable. She worked after hours when necessary, and in time it seemed to her almost as though the business were her own, so much did she give to it of time and energy.

Her whole life was centered in what was essentially her child-parent attitude toward her employer. He often said to her: "When I make my will, I'm going to include you. My business has succeeded partly because of your sympathy and help. There have been many times when I couldn't have got along without you."

But he died suddenly without leaving a will. The business soon changed hands, a new president took charge, bringing in his own assistants, Elsie was relegated to a minor position, and finally resigned. She had saved enough to live on.

Following her employer's death, she was assailed by a sense of guilt as she found herself becoming critical of Providence for dealing harshly with her. She began to have a compulsive urge to say critical things about God, at the same time feeling that they were blasphemous. Her dilemma grew; she felt unforgivable and hopeless. Previously a bright and cheerful person, she became morose and lonely.

All of her life she had been living on an emotional basis that was essentially infantile. When she was young and full of energy, her adjustment to difficulties was fairly easy, but as the years went by this energy naturally lessened. With the death of her employer and the advent of the new president, she found herself unable to carry on with her small emotional and spiritual income. She was virtually without friends, without other interests than employer and job, and she was not making use of the talents and qualities with which she had started out years before. Her religious life was purely perfunctory.

No wonder she finally came to feel a kind of hatred for this inner bond—her unconscious child-parent entanglement—which had kept her from normal living. It was the three-year-old's "I hate you! I hate you!" in adult terms. But while the resentment of a child is projected at an actual flesh-and-blood person, her resentment became turned on the "fantasy father" she herself had created in her unconscious mind. This "fantasy father" received its embodiment in her employer, a father, moreover, who had finally rejected her. And since God is in the unconscious mind as a father, her resentment moved to this ultimate objective.

Similar to Elsie A.'s unconscious creation of a "fantasy father" as an outlet for her emotional self was the behavior of Charles C., who in childhood was so closely attached to his mother that in adult life each woman with whom he came to be involved in any way became a "fantasy mother." Married twice, he had each time demanded such an all-enveloping mother love from his wife that no woman could have met the requirements.

Although C. was critical and rebellious when his wife failed to minister to him as to a child, there developed within him at the same time a deep sense of guilt at demanding this mother-child relationship. He dimly realized that he was trying to make his wife act as though she were a mother to him. In such cases the individual with such an unconscious childish impulse feels a desire to punish himself. He has been taught that it is wrong to remain on this childish level beyond childhood, and therefore the conscience demands punishment.

The capacity for self-criticism is inherent in human beings, and is developed by the parental attitude toward the growing child. The distinction between wise and unwise comes early in life, but the things to be termed right or wrong are varied by training. The child's conscience is based on an acceptance not so much of the outward attitudes of his parents as of what he feels to be their inner consciences.

A certain woman was, as a child, in a family that belonged to a small religious sect which did not believe in bright clothes or jewelry. Even wearing a wedding ring was forbidden. After this woman left her home, she abandoned these beliefs, and began to wear gay colors and jewelry, but she admitted that she never put on a bright-colored dress or a necklace—even after a score of years—without a twinge of guilt.

Another example of this "carry-over" conscience is found in a man who was reared in a strict Scotch-Presbyterian household where Sunday observance barred cooking. Years later he confided that whenever he sat down to a good Sunday dinner with friends he always had a feeling that somehow he was doing wrong.

These examples involve more or less superficial matters, but they do show that the way the twig is bent in infancy, so does it tend to grow in the adult. The early relationship of children to their parents gives rise to the infantile conscience and sets the pattern for the reactions of adult life.

The child finds security and the bulwark of his existence in love. He has an overwhelming need for being loved. He early interprets the unspoken as well as the expressed attitude of his parents to indicate pleasure or displeasure, approval or disapproval, toward his behavior. Thus is the conscience born. The child's adoption of his parents' attitude creates this budding conscience. The child's anxiety may be termed the earliest form of the conscience.

Freud said: "The institution of conscience was at bottom an embodiment, first, of parental criticism and subsequently of that of society."

The child, in the process of socializing himself, often develops a profound sense of wrongdoing. Most of us will agree that it is quite unnecessary to give a child a sense of wrongdoing in order to make him become a social person. Yet there is hardly a child who does not acquire this sense of wrongdoing, much or all of it about things that have nothing to do with sin.

A group of nursery children, aged two to four, were asked what would happen to them if they were "naughty." Every one of the twenty-five was aware of the meaning of the word "naughty."

As time goes on, comments, censures and prohibitions, in short, the attitudes of the parents, become transformed in the child's mind into unchangeable, fundamental laws of right and wrong, and, unless this growth of the conscience is wisely guided, the result will be serious conflict. The child-conscience which demands punishment for things that are not really wrong can consume so much energy and create so much tension as to cause a reaction which may in reality be an offense against society. Excessive drinking, for example, may be brought about by the unbearable tension of the conflict between normal impulses and a misguided childish conscience which acts as a barrier to them.

In the process of conscience building there are four phases:

(1) A primitive impulse of love.
(2) A profound need for holding the parents' love, and for being obedient to them.
(3) A synthesis of the childish impulse for self-criticism with the parental criticisms.
(4) The modification of all of these feelings by the contact with life.

Dr. Thomas R. was reared in a deeply religious family. His father was a gentle, almost saintly person. As the young man went through college and on to the study of medicine, he became more and more critical of his father's religious belief, and finally rejected it altogether. But his early faith in it was not to be so lightly discarded. At the height of his professional career he began to suffer from a morbid anxiety over his work. He was teaching in a medical school at the time and his morbidity took the form of a sense of guilt toward the head surgeon. He felt that he was not doing his duty toward him. His morbid anxiety grew to such a degree that it would make him go back to the ward several times at night to see that nothing had been neglected. His perturbation became so great that it seriously interfered with his work and impaired his health.

An analysis of his anxiety showed that what he worried about was not his duty toward his chief, but his failure to live up to his father's ideals.

We are told many things as children—especially about certain aspects of "right" and "wrong"—which as adult, reasoning beings we discard, or at least modify, in the light of experience in the world of reality, as distinct from the infantile world, and so grow and broaden. Actually, of course, the voice of conscience can never be shut in. If an individual tries to do this ruthlessly and utterly, he will turn to anti-social acts in an effort to escape his own inner dictates. Shakespeare demonstrates this in the character Macbeth, who, having once disregarded his conscience by committing murder, had to continue on his bloody course.

The mind goes, in a normal progression, from the dominant parent image of childhood to a conception of God as an omnipresent, almighty, universal Parent who watches, guards from harm, and punishes transgressions. Religion and psychiatry agree about this.

There is a precept inherent in all religious teaching, that if an individual seeks to better his life, there is definitely a way to do it. First, there must be a conviction of sin or wrongdoing. Second, there must be repentance, or a desire to lead a better life. Third, restitution must be made to whomever has been injured or treated badly. Fourth, there must be atonement, self-punishment of some kind or other. Finally, the average person arrives at the point where he feels forgiven. He is then able to take up life again. Obviously, no one can go through life carrying the ever-mounting burden of a disapproving conscience.

Stevenson phrased it thus: "Day after day we must thumb the hardly varying record of our own weakness and folly." For some, repentance and prayer make it unnecessary to keep that record "hardly varying."

There are others, however, whose unconscious impulses or wishes violate their infantile consciences, so that they are never quite able to feel really forgiven. There are certain conditions which make a peaceful resolution of the pain inflicted by a sense of guilt difficult and often impossible. The adult reasoning, the adult conscience, may consent to the reasonable thesis that repentance and resolution are adequate, but the infantile unconscious conscience may reject it.

"When you have wished to do a thing, then you have done it," says the unconscious mind. And so to some people the crime, which was only wished and hence is imaginary, cannot be atoned for. They are impelled to go over and over the formula of being convicted of sin, of repenting, of deciding to lead a new life, of making restitution (actual or psychological), of atonement (often self-punishment), and then instead of attaining a sense of peace and of freedom from anxiety, they begin all over again. Some even go so far, in their necessity for self-punishment, as actually to commit indiscretions or wrongdoing *in order to have this objective excuse* for the sense of guilt for which they are unable to assign the correct cause.

Dr. William Healy, who did so much for maladjusted children in the juvenile courts of Boston and Chicago, observed that children with a repressed sexual urge often turn to some objective form of wrongdoing, such as stealing, in order to be punished for their secret "sin." They can understand and endure the punishment for theft, but the demand for punishment for the inner sense of guilt is more than they can stand.

Inability to arrive at a sense of forgiveness for unconscious impulses often results in morbid states of mind. Individuals who are virtuous and kind are sometimes completely possessed by a sense of guilt which they cannot shake off or repent away. They need to learn the workings of the unconscious mind which develops this morbid sense of guilt that makes them so unhappy. Without this understanding, religion is often of no avail.

Conscience and the Sense of Guilt

NORMAN VINCENT PEALE

A MAN CAN STAND A LOT AS LONG AS HE CAN STAND himself." So declared the famous writer, Axel Munthe. "He can live without hope, without books, without friends, without music as long as he can listen to his own thoughts." Because this is so patently true, the wise thing, the absolutely necessary thing for every man to cultivate at all costs, is a *self* with which he can live in peace and happiness. He must look to his conscience and eradicate the sense of guilt.

One thing is sure: whether you like it or not, you have to live with yourself. Goethe once said, "Beloved brother, let us not forget that a man can never get away from himself."

Lord Byron, when fleeing from England, heartbrokenly asked: "What exile from himself can flee?"

Indeed, it is a fact that a man may flee from other men and from familiar scenes and the obligations of life, and may even become a recluse in an obscure corner of the earth; he may turn his back on the social conventions and on early training and beliefs; but from himself there is no escape. I saw in a newspaper an account of a young man who was attempting to flee after having done a great wrong. He traveled the world over, but finally said pathetically, "Everywhere I go I am still myself, and I myself am the penalty for the wrong I have done."

This is one of the inescapable facts of life—you have to live with what you are. For some this may be described as heaven; for others, it is literally hell. For some it is romance; for others it is an intolerable boredom. In some men happiness and delight well up out of their hearts. They are alive and vibrant with the sheer joy of living. Life for them is an ever-fresh adventure. Every morning means a fresh beginning, every evening brings the deep satisfaction of a day richly lived. Such men are constantly finding within themselves unexplored riches and fresh sources of happiness. It is a joy to live with a self like that.

There are other men for whom it is not so. They have divided and conflicting personalities. In them is a contentious internecine spirit. They are at odds with themselves most of the time. They are like one of the characters in a modern novel about whom the author says, "He was not a personality, he was a civil war." Theirs is a self which desires to do right, but all too readily acquiesces in evil. Theirs is a self, stung by remorse and haunted by a sense of guilt over past misdeeds. Theirs is a self which is horribly conscious of self because it is concerned only with self. To live with a self like that is hell. Nor is there any evasion, any escape. We have to live with what we are.

In light of this grave and inescapable fact it becomes evident that the supremely important thing is to develop a self with which we can live satisfactorily. Since whether we like it or not we do have to live with ourselves, we profoundly want to become good company for ourselves. We want to be able to enjoy the self we have to live with.

When my little daughter Margaret was about five years

old, I was awakened one morning by the sound of her childish voice in the nursery next to my room. It was about six o'clock, and she was carrying on a great conversation with herself, interspersed with bubbling laughter.

I went into the nursery and interrupted the monologue by saying: "Margaret, this is a strange time for you to be talking so noisily to yourself. You are disturbing everyone who is trying to sleep in this house. Furthermore," I continued, "it seems to me rather foolish for you to lie there talking to yourself and laughing at your own remarks."

"Oh, Daddy," she said, in that tone with which children immemorially have put their parents in their proper place, "Oh, Daddy, you don't understand. I have an awful good time with myself."

I have often reflected on that statement. It not inappropriately describes a fundamental factor in successful living.

We should remember that this business of building a self is something at which we are constantly working. We are not born with a complete self. Nature endows us with only a nucleus, only the potentials.

The soul becomes apparent only as it develops. We are continuously building up or breaking down the self with which we were born. Through the years every thought, every emotion, every experience contributes to the quality of the self. No matter how old we are, or how set we may be, our self is in the making. We are always in the continuous process of creating the self we have to live with. Everything contributes to its greatness or littleness. You will remember Tennyson's discerning remark, "I am part of all I have met." By the same token everything we have met is part of us.

Winifred Rhodes, the helpful writer, expressed it in a

great phrase, "Life's greatest achievement is the continual remaking of your self so that at last you know *how* to live." This process of self-development is expressed in such everyday remarks as: "How he has grown!" or "He is not the man he used to be."

These remarks represent a statement of the fact that we are constantly changing, whether for good or bad.

How can we go about developing a self we can live with happily, a self free from the domination of a wounded conscience and a sense of guilt? We could indulge in much theory and speculation at this point, but a more effective method is to analyze an actual specimen in the laboratory of life. Let us take a man who had tremendous difficulty living with himself, but who solved the problem so effectively that he became thinker, philosopher, and leader in the Christian Church, Paul, the Apostle. He was a man who, by his own admission, suffered acute inner conflict and division. He once cried, "O wretched man that I am! who shall deliver me from the body of this death?"

That is a very graphic description of inner conflict. He evidently had trouble with his good intentions too, for he complained that "The good that I would I do not: but the evil which I would not, that I do." But he won his fight with himself, and finally at the end of a life of heroic proportions, great in achievement but studded with pain, shipwreck, stonings, beatings, and prison, ending in martyrdom, he was able to say: "I have fought a good fight, I have finished my course, I have kept the faith." The man who said that was a man at peace with himself, who had developed a self with which he could live with profound inner contentment.

And what was his secret? It is expressed in these

words, without which no explanation of this great life is possible: "I live; yet not I, but Christ liveth in me." That is to say, his life was now centered not in his divided and inharmonious personality, but in Christ, in whom are no divisions nor conflicts. Christ became the center around which his personality organized itself, and so the divisions in Paul's personality were healed and he became a self with whom it was pleasant for him to live.

What took place in Paul's life to work this transformation which may likewise be applied in your life and mine? The secret can be simply stated. Paul became a religious man, which is to say that he put his life in God's hands. He tried to live according to the highest idealism as taught by Christ. He never compromised from that time on with what he knew to be right. He found in religion the key to a pleasant relationship with himself. He discovered that if he lived according to the principles and spirit of Christ, he would have peace of mind because his mind was clear.

Psychiatrists are now saying what the ministers have always said, that a clear mind, free of, or forgiven for wrongdoing, is essential to the harmonious organization of a man's personality. Marcus Aurelius, one of the world's wisest men, knew the truth of these things. "The one thing worth living for," he declared, "is to keep one's soul pure." A healthy mind is Christ's contribution to men. Faith in Him eliminates that sense of guilt which interferes with a healthy mind.

A man who came to see me one day asked if, as a modern minister, I still believed in the old Victorian ideas of religion. He asked me if religion had been emancipated to the point where it admitted that it had been wrong about the "old moral prohibitions," as he called them. I told him the Church still believed that sin is sin, and that one of the truest things ever said is that "the wages of sin is death." Thereupon he started a tirade against the Church in general and ministers in particular. He said that he had cast "all those beliefs" aside and that he was perfectly happy. He came back at least a dozen times in the ensuing days and vehemently reiterated his insistence that he had been happy ever since he had cast aside the old moral restraints.

It was easy to see that, far from being happy, he was in the utmost mental misery. In violently condemning the Church and its ministers, and declaring that he had cast aside his beliefs, he was pathetically trying to rationalize his sins. As a matter of fact, he was really berating himself. I sat looking at him and reflecting upon the enormous unhappiness that can come to a man by sinful living. What a tangle his mind was in! What pressure was bearing down on his soul! I thought of Morley's apt phrase in which he describes sin as "those terrible impedimenta which rest upon the soul." If I could have said to the man at that moment, "You can leave your self here and walk away without it," I should have had his everlasting gratitude. But no man could do that for him, nor could he do it himself. He had developed a certain kind of self and he had to live with himself. There certainly was no happiness for him.

But as a minister of the Christian religion I was able to tell him how he could change that inescapable self into a self with which he could live in happiness. I quoted these words from the Bible to him—words with which St. Paul expressed what he had discovered in his own experience: "If any man be in Christ, he is a new creature: old things are passed away; behold, all things are become new." He listened and then I heard him saying to himself reflectively: "Old things are passed away . . ."

I said, "That would be wonderful, wouldn't it?" He nodded.

"You have no idea," he fervently declared.

To make a long story short, this man in the Twentieth Century did what Paul had done in the First Century. He became converted, accepting Christ in his own life. If you could see how happy he is today, you would realize that when I say Christ has the power to change the worst kind of self into a glorious self, I have spoken the most important personal truth that it is possible to utter.

In order to control conscience and be free from the burden imposed by a sense of guilt we must practice the good. But before we can practice the good we must definitely know what the good is.

As a clergyman I have frequently been asked to explain what is the meaning of the concepts "good" and "bad." What are right and wrong? Evidently, there is widespread bewilderment on this point. This represents a change from past years, for our fathers recognized a clear demarcation between good and evil. That clear line has been blurred in our time. The contemporary mind seems to experience difficulty in knowing the bad from the good. A wide gray area of uncertainty exists in which the black and white are strangely mingled. Ours is an age of moral confusion. We are at one of those cynical junctures of history where men have discovered the almost rightness of a great deal that is wrong and the almost wrongness of a great deal that is right. To be sure, the person oriented in the spiritual life is not troubled in this way, but as spiritual expertness is not a widespread attainment, the question of what is right and what is wrong needs some clarifying.

It is a hopeful sign that there is a growing desire, especially on the part of youth (which is fundamentally decent and square-shooting), for a surer basis of morals, to fit our generation as effectively as did our fathers' code in their time. Is the old code still valid or do we need a revision?

In view of this growing desire we must do more than merely tell people to be good. We must enlighten them as to what good is. They must be taught how to discriminate clearly between right and wrong and thus avoid falling into moral compromise, which is responsible for the sense of guilt that clouds the happiness of so many people today. They must be shown that apart from the superficialities set up by some as religious conceptions there does exist a certain immutable and timeless morality. The requirements of society do affect our morals. For instance, the high crime of the old West was horse-stealing, for the reason that a man's life often depended upon his horse. Without a horse on the vast plains, he was at the mercy of Indians, buffalo stampedes, thirst, hunger, and other hazards. In an industrial civilization with abundant transportation, car-stealing is much less a moral offense than improper working conditions for employees, or stock manipulations in which thousands of small investors are ruined.

In any society and under any conditions, however, some moral principles are basic, growing not out of ephemeral requirements of society, but out of the immemorial experience of mankind. As James Russell Lowell says:

> "In vain we call old notions fudge,
>   And bend our conscience to our dealing;

> The Ten Commandments will not budge,
> And stealing will continue stealing."

We must also realize that it is not only possible to live the good life but that it is indeed good to do so. Also, we must urgently emphasize that a sense of guilt acquired either through ephemeral morality or real guilt about real sins may be entirely eliminated. A man must *know* he can look directly at his sin and be finished with it. He must know that he is forgiven, and then be able to go about the business of living with a light heart.

A middle-aged woman came to ask my advice about a trivial domestic matter. As we talked, it became plain that she was thoroughly unhappy and that her misery was rooted in some deeper cause than the trivial domestic matter. After several conferences, with a deeply ashamed and thoroughly beaten look, she confessed that a grievous sin lay upon her conscience. This sin was a deep center of infection in her mind.

After observing many such cases we come to a realization that sin is more than a theological concept. To look upon it as a mental infection is much nearer the truth. Sorrow wounds us, but it is a clean wound and heals in normal fashion. Sin, however, is like a splinter of infectious shrapnel received in battle. Whereas a soldier's body may be pierced by clean shrapnel which will come to be solidly surrounded by healthy flesh, an unclean fragment will be a source of infection, causing various troublesome symptoms until removed. So, if a man commits a sin, his mind attempts to rationalize and justify it, in effect to insulate it, but in vain. As the sin sinks deeper into the mind, the infection spreads. Sometimes the result is a nervous breakdown twenty or forty years hence, or perhaps much sooner than that; the color and pleasure of life are drained out because the infection has attacked the spiritual center, even as a physical infection may attack the body tissue.

The woman mentioned above confessed her sin to me in my capacity as a minister of religion, it being her belief and mine that I acted for God. A sin may of course be confessed directly to God in prayer through faith, but experience has proved that it is more effective to confess a sin to God through another person who is trustworthy and understanding.

I prayed with her, asking God to receive her confession and forgive her. She too prayed for forgiveness. A sense of peace came over her, partly caused by the relief of getting her sin off her mind, but it went deeper than that. Christ explains it, "My peace I give unto you: not as the world giveth, give I unto you." It was God's peace, the deep joy of Divine forgiveness which came to this woman.

Even then she could scarcely believe it. She had carried the sin so long it was difficult for her to accept deliverance. Perhaps also her sense of guilt had lain so heavily upon her that it was inconceivable to her that it could be lifted. That it *was* lifted seemed too good to be true! So she began to take her guilt back again. God had forgiven her, but she was not going to forgive herself. Only by the most earnest consultation and prayer was she brought to the point where she stood up to her forgiven sin and said, "I am through with you for good and all."

After this finally happened she said to me one day, "Now I can sing again." I then recalled that she had told me that in her earlier days she so bubbled over with the joy of life that she was forever singing, but that finally the songs had died away. How could she sing with a weight like that on her heart?

"Now I can sing again," she said, when I had told her she could forget her sin, and she finally believed me. I have seen real religion do that times without number—it sets people to singing again by lifting that heaviest of all burdens, the sense of guilt, from the soul.

Among the methods of determining whether an action is right or wrong is your own sense of moral discrimination. We have an instinctive sense of what is right without being told. Jesus said, "Why even of yourselves judge ye not what is right?" St. Paul said, "He that is spiritual judgeth all things." That is to say, the spiritually sensitive person is not confused but judges accurately. Time after time men asked Jesus, "What shall I do?" and he countered with the query: "What do you think?"

There is a "true Light, which lighteth every man." Get a man to be perfectly honest and he knows by an inner light what is right and what is wrong. A man who came to see me asked if, under certain circumstances "over which he had no control," what is called immorality might not be "all right." He argued in favor of it and then asked for my answer.

I said, "What do you think?" and after a long pause, he replied, "You are right."

A politician associated with a bad crowd came in and rather vehemently and nervously defended certain men whose graft had become known. He talked so loud I thought of Emerson's subtle line, "The louder he talked of his honor the faster we counted our spoons." His loud speech was the effort to drown out his conscience, and I was not surprised later to see his name listed in new disclosures.

In part, this instinctive knowledge of right and wrong is the result of centuries of Christian teaching. Dr. Albert Schweitzer, who has spent years in tropical Africa as a physician, tells us that the savage Negro also reveals an instinctive response to good. He seems to know good at once when he sees it, which would indicate that it is a basic reaction rather than an ethical hangover or the superimposed customs of religion. Indeed, religion may be regarded as the formal statement of an instinctive good in human nature which is as natural as hunger.

Mark Twain, in *Huckleberry Finn,* perhaps spoke a profound truth when he said, "The moral sense may take up more room in us than all our insides put together." We know what is right when we stop deluding ourselves.

Right may also be determined on the basis of results. Is wrong workable? Is it sensible? Seneca wisely declared, "If thou wouldst bring all things under subjection, subject thyself to reason." Jesus said to the man who sinned, "Thou fool, this night thy soul shall be required of thee."

Men afterward say, "I was a fool to have done that." It is not "the morning after" that is most tragic, but "the years afterward."

Religion and psychiatry working together as a result of long experience with people who are paying the piper, say of sin, "It was not wise to do this." It is a truism that what is wisest is best; therefore the wise is the good, the unwise is the bad. Scarlett O'Hara, in *Gone With the Wind,* despairingly said, "Oh, it seemed so right when I did it, but it was all so wrong. If I had it to do over again, I'd do so differently."

A good skill to develop is a capacity for moral previewing, the ability to foresee the result; to project the mind ahead and see how a thing will look after it is done.

A man thinking about committing a sin would do well to imagine reading about it as if it had become public.

The teachings of Christ are the surest test of what is good and bad. He declared he came to give men the "abundant life"—that is, a life of peace, happiness, and satisfaction. In his teaching he outlined the way to attain this "blessed life." In the Sermon on the Mount, in the fifth chapter of Matthew, he succinctly outlines the way to be happy. "Blessed (happy) are the pure in heart." "Blessed are they which do hunger and thirst after righteousness," and down through an impressive list of virtues, each of which is a vital element in the happy life.

At the end of the Sermon on the Mount, the Master concludes with the dramatic alternative, "Therefore whosoever heareth these sayings of mine, and doeth them, I will liken him unto a wise man, which built his house upon a rock: and the rain descended, and the floods came, and the winds blew, and beat upon that house; and it fell not: for it was founded upon a rock. And every one that heareth these sayings of mine, and doeth them not, shall be likened unto a foolish man, which built his house upon the sand: and the rain descended, and the floods came, and the winds blew, and beat upon that house; and it fell: and great was the fall of it. And it came to pass, when Jesus had ended these sayings, the people were astonished at his doctrine: for he taught them as one having authority, and not as the scribes." Those who heard these words knew instinctively that Jesus was talking about the Truth—it is wise to do what is right and foolish to do what is wrong. One means security; the other, collapse.

A primary function of religion, and I believe of psychiatry too, is to point the way to happier living by teaching men and women how to cope with a sense of guilt.

Psychiatry uses its own methods of diagnosis and treatment.

Religion brings to distressed minds the knowledge of God's forgiveness and thus the peace that passeth all understanding.

FIVE:
Self-criticism, Failure, and Success

Self-criticism, Failure, and Success

SMILEY BLANTON

IT MAY SEEM PARADOXICAL, BUT THE MORE CONSCIEN-
tious and highly civilized a man is, the more likely he is to
want to fail—to love to lose. This excessive unconscious
sense of unworthiness and morbid self-criticism, with the
unconscious attendant efforts at self-injury, is perhaps the
least understood aspect of the sense of guilt. In order to
understand it we need to know the nature not only of the
sense of guilt but also of the consequent desire for punishment.

Here, as in all studies of the motives of human behavior, we must lay aside those everyday criteria for thinking
which concern only the conscious mind.

When Edward T. came to the pastor's study for consultation and help, he was a broken man, nearly spent. He
had exhausted his strength in what seemed a hopeless
struggle for existence. He was a failure, physically ill,
mentally depressed. He wondered whether some unkind
fate pursued him, or a punishment was being meted out
by God for his sins.

His story, as he told it to the pastor, was as follows:

His father was a stern, upright, hard-working man who
had come to this country from Europe and had founded a
drugstore in a small town. The town grew and the store

prospered so that by the time Edward was a young man his father had established three branches in neighboring towns.

Edward was one of two children. His sister married and left home; he went to college and made a brilliant record. His specialty was history; he hoped to teach it, but upon his graduation his father asked him to enter the business with him and eventually take charge of it.

His father recounted how hard he had worked to found his business and how it had grown under his efforts. He pointed out that he had no one to leave it to except his son, and that if his son did not accept the responsibility, it would pass into other hands upon his retirement and perhaps go to pieces. In conclusion, he flatly told his son that he thought it was his duty, in view of all that he had done for him, to give up his ambition to teach and come into the store.

For a while Edward was torn by the conflicting emotions, but finally gave way to his father's urgings, dropped his plans for a teaching career, and entered the business. But he hated the store because it symbolized his frustration; and his hatred included an antagonism toward his father who had forced him down a road he did not want to follow.

Nevertheless, he was very conscientious and a hard worker. Actually, the more he hated the work, the harder he applied himself to it. He spent long hours at it, mastered the details of the business, and became an efficient assistant to his father. Twenty years passed and Edward T.'s father suddenly died. Then, despite his valiant efforts, the branch stores began to do badly after a few years; two of them failed, and the third was sold at a loss.

Then the main store began to show signs of slipping.

He seemed unable, somehow, to pick competent help when the older employees dropped out; a lunch counter which he put in at great expense failed, and, finally, after much worry, he was forced to sell at a big loss. The man who bought the store proceeded to make a fortune out of it.

Edward T. established a store in a neighboring town, and finally took in a partner. This partner, whose record he had never really investigated, was a shrewd chap and turned out to be crooked. One day federal officers arrested him for selling alcohol for bootleg purposes. Edward T. spent all the money he had left getting himself out of the unpleasant situation that followed the partner's arrest.

He went to work for others, but his periods of employment were widely spaced by stretches of idleness. By the time he came to consult the minister he had long been destitute. The nervous and mental strain that he had been under for years had reduced him to chronic fatigue and illness.

It is clear that Edward T.'s failure was not due to any external fault but to his own unconsciously-motivated actions. He brought a strong hatred to the business that was to be his lifework. This antagonism and the anger toward his father who had coerced him into the business resulted in an unconsciously engendered sense of guilt. Year by year, as he realized his psychological unfitness for the career, his anger and antagonism grew until unconsciously, to punish himself for his hatred of his father, he began to want to fail, even at the cost of great self-injury. That is exactly what did happen.

Robert S. was an attorney for a company that installed

electrical equipment. He had a strong suspicion that the company president was dishonest, that he often cheated his customers. Whenever there was litigation, however, S. accepted the president's word, since he had no real evidence of dishonesty. He served as attorney for this man's firm for five years, with an annual retaining fee of ten thousand dollars. Then he discovered what he considered proof of his client's dishonesty and severed the connection.

But long before, prodded by his unconscious sense of guilt at taking this money, he had set out to "balance the books" in his own mind in regard to that retaining fee. Whenever he got the chance to spend the fee through a foolish investment, he did so. His sense of guilt prevented him from using the same judgment in investing it as he did other moneys earned.

Sometimes our unconscious sense of guilt is more clever than our conscious selves in making us fail. For example, we may get ourselves a job which we are perfectly capable of doing well but which makes us unhappy; we stick to it despite the fact that we know it is not the work we should be doing. Conscience keeps us at the grind but failure gives us a way out.

Kay P. wanted to write, and as soon as she left college got herself a newspaper job. The only available position on that paper was assistant to the society editor. A year later the society editor resigned and Kay became the head of her department. She did her work so well that she won both praise and pay increases. But she hated her job. It was not the kind of writing she wanted to do, and she hated the teas and weddings and other events she had to attend, and she hated the constant pressure on her to put things in the paper which she considered stupid and irrelevant.

When she talked of resigning, her friends all said: "How foolish! You have a good job, you have good pay, you are secure. What else *do* you want to write?"

She didn't know exactly; but she did know that it wasn't society news.

Time passed and her annoyance grew. She began to make mistakes in her reports of events and in names in the society columns. Then she began to overlook or leave out important news. She was warned by the managing editor, but to no avail. The climax came when she confused the principals in an important wedding with a prominent couple about to get a divorce.

A mistake like this could only have been a deliberate effort of her unconscious will to fail. It succeeded: she was discharged. Depressed by the blow that had fallen, she came to consult the minister in the church clinic. Was she inadequate, useless? she asked. When her repugnance to her job was discovered, she was asked, "If you could rub an Aladdin's lamp and have the kind of work you'd like to do, what would it be?"

"I would like to write radio scripts," she replied, "and I believe I could do it."

She finally found such work, and after a few months was happy and on the way to success.

It must be clear that in the case of this woman her unconscious mind did know better than her conscious mind, for if she had not made a whole series of mistakes, she might have kept on being a society editor for life, despite the fact that she disliked her work.

There are men and women who fail because the program they have set for themselves is impossible of fulfillment: because the program itself represents a fantasy rather than a reality.

Robert G. was a brilliant young dentist who happened to settle in a small town where, in order to become a professional success, he had to succeed socially. But he was so shy that he blushed when a stranger spoke to him; so awkward that he danced badly. His hobby was bird study, in which field he was something of an expert. It became his only solace when all his efforts to succeed in social life failed.

It would seem reasonable to expect that all these people, viewing each his own conduct, would be able to recognize their weakness, would be, as we say, rational about it. What kind of thinking made them fail to see the obvious in their behavior? As a matter of fact, they did see the obvious in their behavior, but they gave it a significance that it did not have. E. T. saw that he was failing in his father's drug business. Unable to admit that he unconsciously preferred to wreck the business and his own life rather than accept his father's demands, he gave himself the explanation that he was being pursued by an unkind fate. He did this primarily because it was too painful to face his anger at and hatred of his father. This kind of reasoning is known as rationalizing; that is, making an explanation appear to be rational when it is not really so. Rationalizing serves to blind us to the true causes of events. It is an expensive and destructive type of thinking—and all too common.

Only when the conscious will and the unconscious will agree can we succeed without inner friction. When the conscious will and unconscious will do not agree, the person is pulled first this way, then that. He is said to have too weak a will, which is an inadequate or false way of stating it, for he may be very strong-willed. The stronger the will is, if it is split, the more destructive will be the result. It is not lack of will power that paralyzes action but conflict between the conscious will and the unconscious and often infantile will.

The remedy lies in insight. It is necessary to understand from just what experience buried in the unconscious mind comes the sense of guilt and with it the will to fail. With insight the conflict can be resolved and the condition remedied.

Every being feels unworthy at some time or other. We are all more or less inadequate to our tasks. This feeling is common to intelligent men although dressed sometimes in the garments of confidence. The sense of inadequacy is one of man's little secrets from man that does not fool the observant. But if the feeling of inadequacy does not coincide fairly closely with the facts, then it is time to institute a little quiet self-examination. A constant sense of unworthiness and failure is potentially dangerous. Incidentally, it is not usually held by the truly unworthy. The criminal rarely suffers from it consciously, even if his activities result from a repressed sense of guilt.

It is necessary to stop often through life and evaluate the meaning of the words "failure" and "success." The successful person has usually evaluated his failures and profited by what he learned. In scientific research the experiment that has a negative result is often as valuable as one having a positive result.

Failures are not personal defeat. It is morbid to consider them so, for they are just the human way of going forward by what is called in psychology the method of trial and error. It is a curious thing that although very nearly everybody can see this in regard to his work, very few are able to accept it as true also of their "spiritual" life.

To be successful one must be willing first of all to learn what he wishes to do. Then, after having gained the consent of his unconscious mind as he has of his conscious mind, he can bend his unobstructed energy to it. Every man has a right to be happy in his own way so long as it is not socially destructive. Too often we are deflected by the will and attitude of other people about what constitutes success.

A brief and very pathetic story was told by a middle-aged man at luncheon one day. He had had a great love of the land. He had dreamed throughout his boyhood of becoming a farmer, and finally on finishing agricultural college he had been given a fine tract of farming land by his father. He had married happily and raised three children to college age and on the night of the graduation of his third child had been sitting on his front porch reviewing his life and thinking of his deep contentment and great success. Suddenly a car stopped at the gate. A neighbor ran up to the door. Oil had been found on the neighbor's land only a few feet from their common boundary line. There was doubtless just as much on his own side of the fence.

His friends, his wife, his children became obsessed with the desire to see him drill for oil. Reluctantly he did so and struck it rich. He says: "I am too rich to do my own farming now. I hire a farmer. My wife is too rich to direct her own household; she has a staff as big and as efficient as the club has. Sometimes in dry weather, sitting on the club porch, I unconsciously worry for fear it won't rain. Then I come to and realize that, rain or drought, that crop of oil will go on. I have never had a really happy day since my neighbor's car stopped at the gate."

It was suggested to him one day that he could easily put that oil money back in the soil in experimental farming. He looked up quickly with a glint in his eye.

"Then I could be rich and work the soil also; have my cake and eat it." In that way he finally made peace between the demands of his social group and his own real interests.

We cannot be content if a ruthless taskmaster either inside us or outside us deflects us from what is the most satisfactory fulfillment of our needs.

Self-criticism, Failure, and Success

Norman Vincent Peale

BEFORE BEGINNING TO WRITE MY SECTION OF THIS CHAP-
ter, I reread the foregoing analysis by Doctor Blanton
while seated on a balcony of the famous Chateau Lake
Louise, in the Canadian Rockies.

Before me lay Lake Louise, one of the most beautiful
in the world. It was once called Emerald Lake because of
its marvelous coloring, sweeping the whole gamut of blue,
green, amethyst, and violet, undershot by shifting kaleido-
scopic tones of green and gold as if some supreme magi-
cian were everlastingly mixing colors in its magic bowl. At
the end of the lake, directly before me, dazzling white,
was the sun-glorified Victoria glacier, flanked by somber
pine-clad mountains with a far vista of snowcapped peaks.

As I read Doctor Blanton's analysis of the vagaries and
conflicts of the human mind and of the way in which
people are caught in the tangled ramifications of the sense
of guilt and their lives spoiled, I could not help thinking
of the startling contrast of these facts with the peace and
strength of the noble panorama before me. That glacier
cradled among those mighty peaks is thousands of years
old. Five hundred feet deep, the vast ice mass moves forward less than three inches a year as if imperturbably un-
concerned with the hurry and excitement of the men who
gaze with awe and wonder upon its white majesty. He

who surrenders to the exalted greatness and silent eloquence of glaciers and mountains finds himself lifted to a
height where many things cease to matter.

From the high trail the luxurious hotel becomes a mere
speck, as do our little hates and jealousies and material
ambitions. From such heights we see life somewhat as
God must view it. This perspective dwarfs even man's
sins. A world war, if you look down from a great enough
height, is only the momentary agitation of ants and as
relatively unimportant, for we recall that "a thousand
years in thy sight are but as yesterday when it is past, and
as a watch in the night."

Once at the Grand Canyon a geologist remarked to a
few of us that if geological time were reduced in scale to a
week, the last second of that week would represent man's
life on this planet.

A man's haunting sense of guilt set over against timeless glaciers and great silent snowcapped mountains serves
to show him how small our sins are compared with the
greatness of God; how foolish it is to allow the memory of
them to destroy our peace and shatter our powers. In this
environment we become aware finally that the chief thing
about us is not the wrong we have done but the greatness
in us that responds to the greatness of nature. The man
who wrote the Psalms had committed many sins, and he
said, "I will lift up mine eyes unto the hills, from whence
cometh my help." His help, he said, came "from the
Lord, which made heaven and earth." The nature of that
help was that amidst the great vistas, even the sins of one
little man seemed relatively unimportant.

This is in no sense meant to minimize moral lapse, but
merely to contrast with the boundless understanding and
help of God.

"Forgetting those things which are behind, and reaching forth unto those things which are before." The secret is to get away from our little, agitated, ego-centered minds and see life from a great height. Cast your gaze up, away from yourself up to God and then go forward with your gaze on him. Then you *can* forget the things that are behind and instead press forward to the things ahead. Get away from yourself by getting mountains and glaciers—and God—into your soul.

Suppose you did do wrong, you are sorry; ask God to forgive you, then forget it. The important thing is not that you did something wrong. Though it was wrong, you did it. You cannot undo it. But *you* are infinitely more important than one mistake, or for that matter, many mistakes. Climb up higher and get a view of yourself. See what you can become. How utterly ridiculous to allow your mind to harp on a wrong once done until your mind can deal with nothing else and everything centers around this now unimportant matter! You are bigger than your sin, no matter how big it may be, or seem to be. God has forgiven you if you have sincerely besought him to do so. He sees your possibilities rather than the sin. You must forgive yourself as God has forgiven you. Say to your timorous frightened mind: "Yes, I sinned. I was wrong, and I confessed it and I straightened it out with God who forgives me." Your sense of guilt cannot stand much of that sort of treatment. Turn your back on it and go on as if it never happened except that you are wiser and deeply grateful to God who gave you victory like this.

If you are a victim of a chronic sense of guilt with its attendant misfortune of excessive self-criticism and the unconscious attempt to punish yourself by desiring to fail, then, frankly, you face a very serious situation. The man thus afflicted is in most cases aware of his serious state but usually does not understand the workings of this personality disease.

Doctor Blanton in the first section of this chapter has described this malady. I am attempting to show how religion can effect a cure and have already indicated the basis of that cure, which is to practice getting the concept of the greatness of God into your mind and, by an act of faith, to take the healing He offers you.

Of course many people, while accepting the validity of what has been said and desiring to act upon it, are nevertheless so weakened by the long poisoning of the sense of guilt that they have no faith in the possibility of overcoming it. This very defeatism is itself a self-punishment, a final sort of self-punishment, a complete yielding to the will to fail, and often, strangely enough, with a certain grim pleasure. They cannot conceive of being able to shake off these shackles and going forward unhampered, confident, and with wholehearted vigor to success in life.

To this spineless acquiescence in defeat, the answer is that not only can your greatest weakness be overcome through religious faith; it can become your greatest strength. Perhaps you are the person who says, "Yes, I understand how certain people can get hold of the thing you are talking about, but it is not for me; you do not realize how great my weakness is." The answer to that is: No matter how great your problem, it is puny and insignificant before God. With God all things are possible. Whether you accomplish them depends upon your faith. The Bible says, "According to your faith be it unto you," and again it states the amazing fact, "If ye have faith as a grain of mustard seed, ye shall say unto this mountain, remove hence to yonder place; and it shall remove; and nothing shall be impossible unto you."

This defeatist-malady is surely a mountain, is it not? But the Bible says, and thousands of people can testify to the truth of it, that faith removes the mountain so completely that truly nothing is impossible for you. Get this fact fixed in your consciousness; you can conquer the sense of guilt, you can overcome even your own unconscious resistance to cure, you can cast out the devastating childish desire to punish yourself by making yourself miserable and making a failure of your life.

A distinguished statesman once said that in his youth he heard one sentence which, through the later years, had done him no end of good. He has, he declared, repeated it frequently all his adult life, and it has proved a marvelous source of strength. The sentence is: "You can become strongest in your weakest place."

It is a good thought and states two important things about you and me. First, it calls attention to the obvious fact that we have weak places and a *weakest* place. Of course we do not like to admit that fact; we prefer to dwell on our strong points. We do not like to be honest with ourselves. A contemporary author tells of a man who had many distressing faults and who was asked if he ever gave serious thought to his defects. The man replied that whenever he sat down to contemplate his shortcomings, he invariably fell asleep. Of course the falling asleep was a convenient method employed by the unconscious mind to escape thinking of unpleasant matters. Slumber was a form of flight from distressing facts and enabled him to preserve his self-esteem.

It is not easy to be absolutely honest with ourselves, due to the process of rationalization. That is, we have a tendency not to be objective in our attitude toward ourselves. We set our minds to work, not upon dealing with the facts as they are, but upon inventing rational reasons for courses of conduct. Our unconscious minds play tricks on us, and unless we severely check our minds they will deceive us, keeping us from being entirely honest with ourselves and from realizing that we have weak places.

Second, the sentence tells us that we can be strongest in our weakest place. It does not say that we may become merely strong in the places where we are now weak, but that we may become strongest in the place which is now our weakest spot. Some of the tribes of Africa believe that when one man vanquishes another, the strength of the vanquished passes into the victor and he thereby becomes that much stronger. When you conquer a weakness, the new strength that lies in that weakness, its power *over* you, passes *into* you. Each time you overcome this weakness you acquire an additional part of its strength. Its strength is diminished with each victory and your strength is correspondingly increased.

The ultimate result is the complete destruction of your weakness and your acquisition of the strength it had over you. When we vigorously set ourselves to overcome a weakness which we recognize, the direct campaign which we wage tends to bring all our forces into play at that point. We concentrate a great measure of strength at our weakest point, making it our strongest.

The process known as "welding" illustrates the thought. Welding is a process in which two pieces of metal are fused at their point of contact, making a joint that is usually stronger than the parent metal itself. Intense heat is applied in fusion at the point of contact. The intense heat and resulting fusion makes the spot that was weak stronger than any other part.

We should keep in mind that the tendency of our personality is to palliate, to excuse and to defend our weaknesses. At times we need to be jarred out of ourselves, so as to see ourselves with such distinctness that our minds will be forced to accept the fact of our woeful weakness honestly. Holding this realization firmly in mind, attack your weakest place with determination and it will become your strongest place. It has always been the genius of the Christian religion to help men become strongest in their weakest place.

When the postman brings your mail tomorrow morning, suppose you were to open a letter and find in it a large check made out to you and signed by one of the richest men in the world. In the accompanying letter this rich man would say that he knew you needed this money and so he was glad to send it to you as an out-and-out gift without any strings attached and that he wanted you to accept and use it and be happy; furthermore, when this amount ran out you knew where to come for more. Now, what would you do with that check?

A wise man would say, "I need this money and this rich man is giving it to me because he has an abundance and it will give him pleasure to help me in this way."

"This is a good check," the wise man would continue to reason.

"True, it is only a promise written on a piece of paper, but the name signed to the check is a good name and is good for the amount." And so the wise man would go to the bank and cash the check.

A foolish man, on the contrary, would hold the check in his hand and dubiously say: "This check looks good and the name signed to it seems to be genuine and I certainly do need the money, but the rich man cannot mean it for me. The bank would not give me the money anyway, so I will just have the check framed and hang it on the wall, where I can look at it now and then and imagine how nice it would be to have so much money."

Can you imagine anything more stupid?

Well now, here is an amazing thing. You have at this moment, right within reach, a much larger check, made out in your name and signed by the richest One in the universe. You have the check, or at least I assume you have. It is only a piece of paper with a promise written on it, but it is made out to you, and the signer is good for the amount promised. Where is this check? Turn to the Bible and you will find it, not once, but many times, and here is the way it reads: "If ye shall ask any thing in my name, I will do it." Those words are in the Gospel of John, and again in St. Matthew: "According to your faith be it unto you." St. Mark formulates the check in these words: "If thou canst believe, all things are possible to him that believeth." And the great promise to pay overwhelming value is continued in these words: "What things soever ye desire, when ye pray, believe that ye receive them, and ye shall have them."

In these promises we have a check made out to you and to me, to our friends, to everybody who will believe, a check payable on the Spiritual Trust and Guaranty Bank of the Universe. Many wise people have received and read this "check" and believed it, and have cashed it and continue to cash it daily, and they are rich in personal power and they bless the world by radiant and useful lives. They have experienced the tremendous power of faith.

Others—poor souls!—read this check, but down in their hearts they do not believe. They think these are just pleasant-sounding pious words, and if by any remote chance the words are true, they are true not for them, but for somebody else. They even buy a nice copy of the "check" bound in beautiful leather with gilt-edged pages—a lovely Bible—and read over this "check" now and then and wish with a sigh they could have the great things it offers, but they do not cash the "check," but go on living on spiritual relief instead of accepting the abundance of power and joy and strength.

The essence of religion is that it releases in a person a power and a force beyond human capacity to generate, by which he may rise to a plane of existence in which he is superior to everything life may bring him. There once lived a Man who had the gift of power to overcome anything the world could do to Him; and through the years other people, through contact with this Man in spiritual communion, have found the same power. Wistfully, we remember that once He said: "Verily, I say unto you, he that believeth on me, the works that I do shall he do also; and greater works than these shall he do." Why are *we* not "doing works" like that? What is wrong? His was a way of living that made weakness and trouble drop away like withered leaves in the fall. Is it a lost art? How shall we find it again?

If the art has been lost to many of us, what can we do? The answer is, go back and examine it at its source. And when we go back and analyze the life of Jesus, the source of His power, and of His Divine energy, we are impressed by His faith in God. He believed God was near to Him, using Him. He believed in God with the faith of a child.

He kept in close contact and communion with God and as a result He was an open channel for Divine energy.

The New Testament tells us and the lives of many people have borne out the truth that we can have the same kind of power Christ had if we have the same faith He had. This is an astonishing assertion, but the Master Himself made it when He said, "He that believeth on me, the works that I do shall he do also."

Our trouble is that our idea of the power of religious faith is too small, too limited. Most of us assume that the tremendous power bestowed by faith is not for us because we are human and therefore imperfect. Jesus, we argue, had insight and strength of will beyond that which we can expect to have. But remember, the gospel is not a message to the strong and wise but to the deeply and earnestly desiring. It is for those who, being weak, turn to God for strength. They come trying to believe, believing yet not believing, but having faith in God's goodness. They seek to get their thoughts into the mood of Christ's spirit, and so, because they are in earnest, though they are weak, God bestows his power on them. He does not ask them to struggle to overcome the obstacles that are too much for them, but simply to believe in him and put their trust in his goodness and sincerely live the Christian life. These are switches which we throw open on the spiritual powerline, and the grace of God flows through like electrical energy.

Many people fail to obtain the gift of God's power merely because they do not trust their own capacity for faith. They assume they have to be very strong, or truly great saints, but that is not the method Christ teaches. "If thou canst believe," he said, "all things are possible." That means, let go of the tension of doubt and fear and look up to Christ out of your weakness and let your life relax in his care. When you let go and allow your spiritual rigidity to disappear, your life will become an open channel through which the empowering grace of God will pour like a freshet into an arid and dusty country after a long drought.

An example from everyday life of the operation of the power of faith is the case of a young man who came to see me and said he had an insatiable appetite for alcohol which was fast destroying his effectiveness in business. His craving was so great that several times he had arisen during the night to get himself a drink. A psychiatrist would probably have diagnosed his case as "the will to fail"—that is, that basically he *wanted* to fail. That is not infrequently the correct assumption in such cases. He wanted me to pray with him, comfort him, and urge him to go out and fight a fight which he confidently expected to lose, and then, having failed, come back for more prayer and more comfort. After he did just that several times, I told him there was no use trying, and advised him not to try. He was amazed at this, and I explained that the gospel really does not urge us to *try* harder, but to *believe* harder. If the gospel did otherwise, it would be only for those of strong will. The only fight it urges is the fight of faith, the struggle to believe.

I assured him that however much he stirred up his will to succeed, he would probably fail because in his unconscious mind he visualized himself as failing. His will might heroically declare, "I will," but at the same time his imagination whispered, "I cannot," and because imagination is stronger than will, his will would lose. He needed to imagine himself not as failing, but as winning. His faith needed to paint that picture firmly on his inner consciousness. So

I asked him to believe by an act of pure faith that he would vanquish his craving—not tomorrow, or sometime in the future, but to believe that, by the grace of God, he was at that very minute freed from its domination.

"According to your faith, be it unto you," said Christ. He asked me if I was certain of that, and I assured him that I was. By an act of faith he accepted the idea, and whatever were the mental operations involved in the process, the fact remains that at the end of a month he told me he had not the slightest desire for alcohol. Now, at the end of a year and a half, he has had no recurrence of the desire. The moral lesion was healed by so great a curative force that no vestige of the disease remained. What struggle, however sincere, could not do was accomplished by the tremendous power of faith in Christ. Any problem of this life can be successfully handled if by faith we open our minds to the power of God.

Many people conceive of religion as something apart from everyday affairs of the world. They think of it in terms of ceremony or ritual or sermons and often it strikes them as being dull or not particularly interesting. Religion may be described in many ways. I like to think of it as a medicine, a healing medicine for the mind. It has a powerful effect on the poisons that infect the conscious and unconscious mind. Its penetrating potency drives deep into those areas of the subconscious where lurk the sources of infection. It hunts down these mental disease germs and destroys them with the powerful heat of its clean life. The reason I as a clergyman am writing a book in collaboration with a psychiatrist is that modern science recognizes that religion is not extraneous to real life, dealing only in form and ceremony, but that it is an effective therapeutic agent.

A noted American physician remarked, "Most people do not need medicine half as much as a good dose of old-fashioned conversion." Conversion means more than getting an old drunk out of the gutter in a revival meeting or a rescue mission, splendid as that is. It also means getting the evil out of his mind, curing him of the sense of guilt, and in short making a new person of him.

Let me tell you about another man. He held a responsible position. He was a sturdy-looking fellow, and unless you knew the tumult and agitation within his mind, you would think him healthy and strong. Beneath many an apparently normal exterior there may rage storms that would amaze us. Thoreau said, "Most 'men live lives of quiet desperation." This man would awaken suddenly in the early morning full of fears of all that might happen to his family and himself. He was also struck with panic at the thought that certain old sins might catch up with him. Several hours of restless tossing would leave him exhausted before the day's work began. His nerves got on edge so that he easily lost his temper and created many unfortunate situations in his relations with people. His entire career was in jeopardy, for the inner stress under which he labored dissipated the energies he should have applied to his work.

He heard a radio talk in which I made the assertion that religious faith had secured remarkable results in correcting nervousness, stress, and anxiety, and had brought peace and power to many distraught lives. He came to me and confessed certain wrongs, and in the sacred confidence of our church clinic there was lifted from his mind and heart the sense of guilt which had been poisoning his soul, mind, and body. Dr. Blanton and I then made him see that God is not a dim theological concept, but is close to us, that he means it when he says, "My grace is sufficient for thee." I urged him to practice believing in God as a little child believes in a kindly father and to put his nerve-torn life in God's hands—to "rest his burdens" on the Lord. He let go of all his anxieties finally in simple faith.

Through the practice of this faith, stress and tension gradually disappeared and today this man has a deep calm and peace at the center of his life. His old efficiency has returned and his life has regained its joyousness. The more we witness such transformations affected by God's intervention, the better we understand what a great psychologist meant when he said, "The trouble with our generation is that it does not appreciate God enough."

SIX:
Grief
and Sorrow

Grief
and Sorrow

SMILEY BLANTON

WHAT IS THE MEANING OF SUFFERING? THE ANSWER must be sought in those mines of wisdom, the Greek tragedies, Shakespeare's plays, and the Bible. The theme is ever-recurrent. It is nobly expressed by Euripides:*

"Had He not turned us in His hand, and thrust
Our high things low, and shook our hills as dust,
We had not been this splendor, and our wrong
An everlasting music for the song
Of earth and heaven!"

It has been the experience of mankind that suffering, nobly borne, enriches the personality and strengthens the character; only, of course, when that suffering is unavoidable; only when it cannot be prevented by human efforts. It must not be self-imposed suffering.

To help the sufferer is the psychiatrist's function; to help him see what the source of his suffering is, and, if it is removable, how to remove it. The psychiatrist, like the minister, brings sympathy and understanding to the task in addition to a specialized knowledge of the mind that

* The Trojan Women of Euripides, Trans. Gilbert Murray, Oxford University Press, New York, 1915, p. 72.

makes it possible for him to aid human beings who might otherwise go down under the burden.

The psychiatrist will consider whether, unwittingly, the suffering is self-inflicted or the unhappiness self-enlarged. If it is, he can analyze and help.

Suffering comes to the average man or woman in many ways. Death, for instance, or separation is an experience common to all mankind. In such a case the mind is pervaded by a monopolizing emotion, and the capacity to love other than the lost one is, for the time being, suspended. There is inevitably mental pain, depression, loss of interest in the outside world, and a lack of desire for the normal activities of life.

But no matter how strong our grief, the love that enveloped the lost object begins after a while to gather around other objects. This is a necessary reaction if we are to go on living. We normally, after a period of mourning, find ourselves capable of loving again.

There are individuals who continue to grieve inordinately over their loss, but they almost always harbor other causes which immobilize theh capacity to readjust. They have either invested the lost object with an intensity of love that was extremely unwise, or they have had unconscious resentment which the infantile conscience seized on and utilized. Among the elements that went into their grief during the period of mourning were morbid self-criticism and self-reproach. Carrying grief forward after the normal time for adjustment has passed is punishing ourselves by exaggerating our sense of guilt.

In certain cases this morbid grief develops into what we may term melancholia.

An instance:

Mrs. Drew's grief over the death of her four-year-old son was naturally profound, but as the weeks passed it did not abate, although there were four other children and a husband to console her and call upon her attention. She continued to withdraw from them and from her friends, and spent most of the day weeping. She burst into tears at any conversation, no matter how remote, that recalled her dead child to her. She was a devout Christian but got no relief from religion.

Three months passed and her pastor came to realize that there must be some morbid obstacle in her mind that kept her grief alive. He asked her to come to the church clinic. She came, but could not talk about her grief, even in a general way, for weeping.

Some new interest had to be found for Mrs. Drew that would temporarily take her mind off her grief before either psychiatrist or pastor could even examine her case with a view to helping her. She was asked if she would come for a few hours each day to help teach a nursery-school class that the church had organized for the children of working mothers. She consented, and carried out her new duties faithfully. After a few weeks of this outlet for her emotion, she found it possible to talk about herself, and told her story.

When she had had four children, the youngest of whom was sixteen, she found she was going to have another. She became resentful and distracted, feeling that the situation would be difficult with her other children so much older. She could not help feeling that the coming child would add too great a burden to her already crowded life.

Mrs. Drew's husband was a successful business man who had to make frequent trips away from home; when he had a vacation, he would go off to his hunting club to hunt and fish. With her other children practically grown, she filled her life with somewhat overscrupulous housekeeping, devoting herself to her home. Her only recreation was occasional golf or cards with her neighbors. Although she went to church regularly, she had few friends there, since she had withdrawn herself very much from church activities. Her life was extremely limited and a new child would limit it even more, but her moral principles would not permit her to interfere with her pregnancy.

This was the situation in which she found herself when her fifth child was coming. She was physically well, but mentally depressed. During the month before the child was born she cried continuously.

But when the baby came, her attitude changed. He grew into a healthy, lovely boy, and she was happy over him. She became more and more attached to him as he grew, centering her life and affection upon him.

During one of her talks at the church clinic, she said: "I didn't realize it, but I had apparently made my boy an outlet for all my love. I was starved for affection on account of the situation at home; my older children didn't need me any more, and my husband seemed to prefer other people for both work and play. I got so I wanted my new baby to stay in my heart for the rest of my life."

Mrs. Drew's conflicting emotions about the child before he was born, and her excessive affection for him afterward, betray the basis of her own blocked and starved emotions. Wishes, to the unconscious mind, are the same as acts, and the unconscious conscience punishes us for wishes just as though they had really been translated into acts. Mrs. Drew's first resentment and antagonism had been interpreted by her conscience as a death wish and, when the child later died, she unconsciously felt responsible. Hence her morbid suffering.

A similar morbid state occurred in the case of Mrs. Z., who came to the church clinic to consult the pastor about a deep feeling of depression following the death of her husband.

She and her husband had had a rather stormy married life over some thirty years. Mr. Z. was hard-working and loyal but had a violent temper, and they frequently quarreled. Mrs. Z. often resented his unreasonableness, but on the whole their married life had enough positive factors in it to make it worth while for both of them.

Mr. Z. finally retired from business, on the advice of his physician, who found he had a heart condition which might bring sudden death if he kept on working. One night two years later he complained of a slight headache. His wife asked him if he wanted his doctor, but he said no. In the morning, when she went to his room, she found him dead.

The cause of his death was a clot in one of the arteries of his heart. This possibility had been foreseen by the doctor. Yet Mrs. Z. upbraided herself bitterly for her imagined neglect of her husband. She felt that if she had called the doctor despite his "No" he might still be alive. The doctor disagreed with her. But she persisted in believing that she was partly responsible for her husband's death and that God would surely punish her.

It is useless to argue with such a person, and a most serious mistake to try to talk him out of his depression. It is even dangerous. *The slightest depression* requires the most expert treatment.

In the case of Mrs. Z. the quarrels with her husband, and the resulting resentment she had felt toward him while he lived, had been very much repressed into her unconscious mind. To other people she insisted that he was an ideal husband, although they all knew about his quick temper. But she could not deceive her unconscious mind, where her resentment, stored up over the years, was interpreted by her infantile conscience as actual acts of aggression toward her husband, so that when he died she felt that she had had an active part in his death.

In depression and melancholia in which grief or mourning has reached a morbid point, there is nearly always present an unconscious sense of guilt, and the former cannot be relieved unless there is some modification of the latter. If such persons are to be helped even by their religion they must have an understanding of the infantile conscience and how it raises unconscious obstacles to their achieving a normal feeling of forgiveness.

Grief, profound and devastating, can spring not only from the loss of loved ones but also from the loss of faith.

It has been observed in the case of primitive peoples, for example, that when their culture has been destroyed by a conquering invasion, and their religious beliefs undermined, they do actually refuse to live, despite the fact that the urge to survive is strong in all of us.

Some of the Indian tribes inhabiting the West Indies died out completely when the Spaniards came and destroyed their culture and enslaved them. Some of the Polynesian tribes in the South Seas dwindled or died out entirely after the whites came bringing oppression and a new culture. Individuals or peoples may survive oppression, but when they lose their faith or their ideals, the resulting depression makes life not worth living.

Another type of loss which may cause melancholia and depression is known to psychiatrists: it is the loss of a fantasy parent which has been dominating the individual's adult life. For all of us there is both an actual parent and an imagined parent.

Mr. Robert J.'s father, an engineer, was away from home much of the time. When he came home, he would tell of his adventures in strange places and he became a great hero in the eyes of the growing boy, who adored him. But whenever he went away again, Robert felt strong resentment. He believed he did not get enough of his father's love and developed an obsessive necessity to make other men play the part that a real stay-at-home father would have played in the life of a small child. For example, he would pester his men teachers to give him the meaning of a word which he could have looked up for himself, or for the solution of a simple mathematical problem.

When he grew up, he went into a business of his own and was fairly successful. But even here this "fantasy-father" interfered with his life and work. When he went to sell his product and the potential customer did not give him an order, he felt depressed and resentful. Instead of taking it all as part of the day's work, he felt as though the customer had rejected him in some special fashion.

Realizing the extent to which this had a hold on him, he came to the church clinic for help. He was brought to see for himself how his trouble sprang from his first attitude toward his father. He responded promisingly to his new knowledge of himself, but complete understanding of his actions brought in its wake a profound depression. While the depression lasted, it seemed to him that in parting with this fantasy of his father he was losing something that he could not bear to live without.

Many of us have these childish fantasies, in one form or another, and the struggle to shake them off is hard. We cling to them as to something vital to our lives. An analogy is the little boy whose pockets are filled with assorted junk—an old knife, a broken whistle, a chipped marble, a piece of string. If someone should say to him, "Give me the junk that is in your pockets and I will give you a new knife, a new marble, a new whistle, and a whole ball of string," he would show his distrust. But that is the way we are all inclined to act when our infantile concepts are threatened.

However, if we are to achieve any kind of happiness, we must follow the example of the Apostle Paul, who admonished the adult man to put away childish things. He did not mean that we should put away simplicity of outlook, childlike capacity for faith; he meant only that we must put away those childish attitudes which we have to outgrow in order to become adult. From time to time as the child grows he puts aside mistaken ideas about people in order to square his attitude with the facts of life. The adult who has unwittingly clung to childish ideas must also put them aside.

From the child's disappointment and grief over a mistaken ideal there is but a step to the disillusionment and melancholy of the adult who finds himself grieving, bitter, and even cynical over a disappointment. When a fantasy has been shattered, something must take its place, or we suffer.

But there is always something constructive to take its place. The difficulty is how to find it. Many people have the idea deeply implanted in their minds that they must make life hard for themselves. With them suffering itself is a religious faith. The person who has normal goals and ideals will still experience enough stress and failure without adding an unconscious sense of guilt to the store. There is always enough chance for pain without that, always the possibility of "quick-coming death and the pangs of the first-born taken." We were given life not only for pain but also for as much as possible of that particular outgoing of the personality which the Beatitudes have defined as love. It "suffereth long and is kind" even to itself.

Grief
and Sorrow

NORMAN VINCENT PEALE

GRIEF AND SORROW FOR DEPARTED LOVED ONES WILL
lift when we realize the new happiness they are experienc-
ing. This may seem a startling statement but I believe it is
true to the facts. We long "for the touch of a vanished
hand, and the sound of a voice that is still!" That is only
natural. But grief sustained abnormally long is illogical in
view of the well-being of those who have gone on. As
Doctor Blanton suggests, protracted grief is evidence of
something wrong in the unconscious mind or it indicates
that we are thinking not of the beloved departed but,
rather, of ourselves. Grief and mourning can be lightened
by a proper understanding of the blessed condition of our
departed loved ones. Thus faith becomes the answer to
the problem of sorrow.

What happens to our dead? A noble passage from the
Bible, from the book of Revelation, answers: "He that sit-
teth on the throne shall spread his tabernacle over them.
They shall hunger no more, neither thirst any more; neither shall the sun light on them, nor any heat: for the
Lamb which is in the midst of the throne shall be their
shepherd, and shall feed them, and shall lead them unto
living fountains of water: and God shall wipe away all
tears from their eyes."

This passage is surely one of the most beautiful in all

literature, but far more important than its beauty is its keen insight into one great truth about human life, namely, the blessedness of the dead and the infinite peace of their existence. We can know very little of a specific nature concerning the dead. As Shakespeare has so well put it in a famous phrase, it is "the undiscover'd country from whose bourn no traveler returns." For our profounder knowledge of the deep and fundamental questions of life and eternity, we fall back upon that book which, while itself not explicit on this subject, opens up little windows of penetrating thought, through which we have flashing illuminations of truth.

It means much to know that our beloved dead are safe in a place of happiness and peace. Each of us watching loved ones slipping into the great unknown, departing with a smile and a wave of the hand, exclaim with Tennyson:

> "Ah, Christ! if it were possible
> For one short hour to see
> The souls we loved, that they might tell us
> What and where they be."

Without engaging in speculation or being academic about this subject, let us simply examine carefully this passage from the Bible for what it has to tell us about the dead. We are told, first of all, that the fundamental needs of life are met and satisfied. We read, "They shall hunger no more, neither thirst any more." Those who knew them here remember vividly their longings which were never satisfied. Some were hungry—physically hungry. God has pity for all the dead who hungered here for the necessities of life. On many a simple stone is written the short and simple record of the poor. There is a deep, dark, human tragedy in the bodies that were never adequately fed or housed, or clothed: who knew only the pinch of poverty and struggle all their days and for whom the joys of life in a material sense were few and paltry. Yet in a deeper sense this statement does not refer to physical hunger, for there is a greater hunger than that. Alfred Noyes, the poet, expressed it when he said:

"I am full-fed and yet I hunger,
What means this deeper hunger in my heart?"

What is that hunger of which the poet wrote and to which the Bible refers? It is an inner, cosmic restlessness. We are not fundamentally citizens of this world, but rather, as the great Russian writer Dostoievski said, "We are citizens of eternity." Perhaps this restlessness, this yearning for the real world of the spirit, was caught and expressed most clearly by William Watson in one of the most remarkable poems, in my humble opinion, ever written in the English language. I have sometimes quoted it to congregations and have felt a stillness like that of summer noon over a country meadow. It has an effect, for a moment at least, as though a thought was expressed so very profound and true that it induced a hush from that Infinite of which we are a part, soothing momentarily our spirits, worn and torn by this life's fatiguing pilgrimage. It is called "World Strangeness." But listen to Watson himself:

"Strange the world about me lies,
Never yet familiar grown
Still disturbs me with surprise,
Haunts me like a face half-known.

"In this house with starry dome,
Floored with gem-like planes and seas,
Shall I never feel at home,
Never wholly be at ease?

"On from room to room I stray;
Yet my host can ne'er espy,
And I know not to this day,
Whether guest or captive I.

"So, between the starry dome
And the floor of planes and seas
I have never felt at home,
Never wholly been at ease."

This deep human hunger which is felt at times by each of us and which, struggling beneath the surface of our lives, gives us a vague restlessness, can be assuaged in this world by living near to God, which is to say, by living near to the element of eternity.

Our dead often evinced a deep, fundamental longing for something which this earth could not satisfy. The Bible tells us that all their hungers have been appeased and all their thirsts have been quenched. "They shall hunger no more, neither thirst any more." They are now "home."

We are told also in this Bible passage that God has thrown his protection over them; "He shall spread his tabernacle over them." It makes us think of a mother coming in at night looking upon her sleeping child, drawing a blanket over him, tucking it in around him to keep him warm and comfortable, then bending down for a light but loving kiss, and stealing out of the room while the child peacefully sleeps. God, with his great tender heart, we are told, will spread his tabernacle over them as a mother watches over a sleeping child. I have always felt that this deep, kindly and protective love, having so universal a place in human hearts, is only a reflection of the love and tenderness of God. Is it not logical to assume that the love which we find in the hearts of imperfect men and women is also to be found in the heart of the Perfect One, our God?

Some years ago I had a friend, a great soul. He was a big man, big physically and big of heart. One stormy night his home telephone rang and the agonized voice of an acquaintance told him of a tragedy he had just experienced. It was one of the most staggering tragedies that can happen to a man—the infidelity of a beloved wife. She had gone, left his home. He was alone in the dawning knowledge that her love for him was a broken thing. Piteously, like a child in the dark, his heart dead within him, he called out for help. My friend immediately got out his car, drove for a good many miles through the storm to this man's home, and found him bowed in hopeless grief. He walked in without a word, went to the broken man, put his great arms about him and said, "Come with me."

They gathered up a few of his belongings and got into the car where the man sat with his shoulder pressed against my bulky friend. The stricken man told me afterward that as they drove through the night not a word was spoken. What could be said? The unspoken attitude of human sympathy had to speak the message, and he said that as he looked upon the strong, kindly face of his friend, lighted by the dim glow of the dashlight and reflected in the windshield, there came over him a sense of peace and protection and calm comfort. My friend had thrown his tabernacle over him. So God, who loves us with an Infinite love, has spread his tabernacle over our dear departed loved ones.

But this is not all of the comforting story the Bible tells about our dead. It also tells us that God has given them life, radiant and beautiful, such as they never knew in this earthly world. God feeds them and guides them unto fountains of living waters of life, and God wipes away every tear from unto fountains of living waters of life, and God wipes away every tear from their eyes. Our loved ones enter at death into that strange country and a great, kindly personality greets them. He feeds them; feeds the deep hunger of their souls. He leads them wondering to great sparkling fountains tossing their radiant waters into the clear sunlight. They satisfy their thirst and it disappears. Then even as a mother takes her wounded child to her bosom and wipes away his tears, so God smiles on our loved ones, fresh from this world of suffering and hardships, and wipes away every tear from their eyes.

Death has always been pictured as a dark angel, as a sinister figure. I wonder if the metaphor of going home to a mother, to a father, isn't a better and more accurate one. I know a man who became overwhelmed with trouble. He is a strong, resourceful man, but life hit him many blows and the going became exceedingly hard. He felt a deep and irresistible desire to go back to his boyhood home and have a visit with his aged mother.

He wanted, somehow, to recapture the enthusiasm and zest of life which had been drained from his spirit. Streaks of gray were beginning to show in his hair, and as Charles Lamb once said, "Our spirits grow gray before our hair," so it was with this man.

He told me afterward that he went back to the old

home, and his mother, like mothers in every age and in every place, wanted to feed him, give him a good dinner such as he used to have. She put food and drink before him and talked to him about old-fashioned intimate family matters. She was slaking his thirst, and feeding the deeper hunger of his life. As he sat at the table, she passed by and put her hands, soft and tender and wrinkled, on his head, as if she knew the burden he carried and the pain that was in his heart, and was trying, as only a mother can, to wipe away the tears from his eyes.

He said that in the quietness of that place peace came over him and a new enthusiasm for living came stealing back into his heart. Our dead have found in the great mother heart and in the great father heart of God the love and understanding we find in a mother or in a loving father here on earth. Their eyes, closed in death, have opened in the light of an eternal home.

So I say to you who mourn, that if we are to believe the Scriptures, and I know that we can believe them, we may be sure that those whom we have "loved long since and lost awhile" are happy and peaceful and contented, for they are in the Father's house and the Father is with them.

Jesus once said, "In my Father's house are many mansions: If it were *not* so, I would have told you. I go to prepare a place for you, . . . that where I am, there ye may be also." This passage reminds us that He is there and wherever He is it cannot be other than a place of beauty and happiness and peace. Thus sorrow is lifted by our faith in the goodness of God.

But there is another and profound source of grief which we must consider. It is very common and subtle, for the average person does not think of it as a deep grief resting upon the spirit, subtracting from life its color and enjoyment. Doctor Blanton is entirely correct in his thesis that deep-centered grief often emanates from a loss of ideals and of faith.

If a man's life is said to be "wicked," that really means it is stale and thin; it is a state of grief. Wickedness is a panicky escape-mechanism for a personality that is worn out on the inside. Consider a heavy drinker for example. What is wrong with him? Unless it is a psychological "block," the chances are that his life is atrophied on the inside, that he has limited resourcefulness and originality and feels that the only release is to turn to "a glass." The trouble with that method, beyond its obviously sad effects, is simply stated—it won't work! It brings more grief. You cannot get radiant life out of a glass. That can come only out of the mind, a mind at peace.

Many people are trying to satisfy deep hungers and do not know how to do it. The only way that has occurred to some is loose living, compromised morality, and even dissipation. But apparently that method is proving a sad disappointment, for in ever-increasing numbers, people, and particularly younger people—for they are still honest and frank—are returning to religious experience as the only sure antidote for boredom. Here is a generation in confusion, having lost its way, not only with regard to its collective economic and social life, but also in individual life. It may be said that multitudes have literally "come to grief" because their ideals have been lost.

What is the answer to this tragic condition? There is only one thinker who has the answer, the wisest man who ever lived, Jesus Christ. What does he have to say? He says, and the statement shows magnificent insight, uncanny genius: "the kingdom of God is within you."

What did he mean by that? Simply that in each of us is God. If we reject him, he is still there in us just the same, for he never rejects us. But unless we give him control of our inward life, even He can do little for us. Weak as we are, we actually have the power to render the God in us ineffective. But the minute a man sincerely says to God within him, "You take control," he instantly realizes the kingdom of God within him, and radiant life begins. The secret of happiness lies in exercising the spiritual power within yourself. Simply say with a whole heart: "God, you are in me—dominate me," and presently your life takes on a new power and aliveness. When Jesus Christ says, "the kingdom of God is within you," He is saying what wise men have always said, namely, that in you yourself is the answer to your own happiness. This is the surest antidote to deep inward grief of the spirit.

One Sunday night a young man in his mid-thirties came to church. He was well-dressed according to the current style and was in every detail the usual type of youngish man of today. He was successful in business and, his friends told me later, popular socially. He lived a life in which ideals were easily violated or compromised. It would not have occurred to him to be otherwise. His habits and practices were determined almost entirely, not by what he particularly wanted to do, but by what everybody else seemed to be doing.

This mode of life began to pall on him and finally became stale and meaningless. He had not been in the habit of attending church services, but a vague and growing dissatisfaction brought him this particular evening. As he listened to the service, a definite feeling of peace came over him. He said afterward, "Life suddenly became clear to me as, when I was a boy, an arithmetic problem suddenly opened up after I had studied over it a long while."

In the weeks that followed, this man turned to a high spiritual idealism. He did not become "holier than thou," or assume a super-piety, but he became a radiant person, drawing happiness from deep inner wells, and now you have only to look at him to know that he has found the secret of supreme serenity. Once he said to me, "The thing that impresses me about the change in my life is that all the while I had, within my own personality, the capacity for happiness, but was making the mistake of looking for it on the outside." The deep center of grief in his nature had been healed. Your kingdom of God, your state of peace and happiness is *within you,* and you can find there the secret of happier living.

It should be remembered that the word "gospel" means "good news." The good news is that you can have that which you most desire, peace of mind and happiness. The recipient of the good news is the truly happy person. Genuine Christian experience so acts upon man's mind that the barriers to the enjoyment of life are removed, and even in trouble and adversity and pain, his inner song sings on. He knows the seriousness and hardship of life, but come what may, there is something which keeps alive the thrill and delight of living. In a profound sense he has gained the ability to enjoy life. He never becomes satiated. Life to him is ever fresh.

The ability to enjoy life is a direct product of the Christian way of life. Christianity says, "Here is a world made by God. Here is the formula by which to live in this world so that it will mean the most to you. The world has its difficulties," says Christian philosophy, "but to follow the principles of Christ—and you will enjoy it—will be an experience of delight and satisfaction." Nowhere does this Christian philosophy say you shall not sacrifice and suffer, but on the contrary, it teaches us that in these very factors the deepest happiness is not infrequently found.

What is there in the practice of religion that endows us with the rare ability to enjoy life, to overcome that grief which is experienced by those who miss the happy way?

The first element is the real presence of God. It is to know that God is ever-present, that God cares for you and will guide you and watch over you. With this great knowledge at the heart of our philosophy, we have a definite center around which to organize our lives. So let the world do its worst—we know God is with us and we are not dismayed. The sense of God's presence steadies us, it gives us an anchor in the storm, and provides a reservoir of personal power. I do not mean that we will get this steadiness merely from some theological idea about God or some vague belief in Deity; but if we live with God as a friend, God will become so real that He will be our sturdy companion day and night. Then, even when the going is hard, our hearts can be happy within us, for we have His assurance.

I know a man who has been overwhelmed with trouble. He has lost most of his money, there has been sickness in the family, and recently the old home in which he had lived for many years had to be sold. He suffered one blow after another, a buffeting by adversity sufficient to break any man, or at least enough to take all the joy out of life. But he had the capacity for handling these hard knocks. He was equipped with internal shock-absorbers which took up the blows. The old calmness and peace is still in him. He will have no nervous breakdown. Life is still good, and despite all his trouble he is happy and content.

His secret? Well, sometimes a look comes over his face which is eloquent and revealing. To him, God's presence is no idle theory, but a realistic fact which he discovered for himself in about as hard an experience as a man can suffer.

Another thing that makes Christianity a sure technique for enjoying life is that it tells us that to get pleasure out of living, we must live a moral life. What is the trouble with loose living in general? Is it merely breaking a set of theological rules? No! The real trouble is that it takes the bounce out of life. Live wrong, and the old fresh delight in life fades. It is taking something into the system which may add zest for the moment. Soon it grows bitter and leaves a bad taste.

The real delight of life is inside, not outside a man. It is in his heart and mind, not in his physical body. A modern sophisticate whom I used to regard as an "up-and-out" rather than a "down-and-out" because he had clothes and money which the down-and-out lacks, is now one of the most thoroughly happy men I know since a change occurred in his character. He has said to me a hundred times if he has said it once, "I would not trade one day of this new life for the forty years of what I used to be before I found that religion can make a man really enjoy life."

Faith is the answer to another manifestation of the grief which is caused by lack of ideals. It reveals to us that when things frequently go wrong, it is not due to outward conditions or circumstances, but more often to the faults which lie within ourselves. Faith gives us keen insight and the ability for honest self-analysis.

Some time ago there came to the church clinic a man about twenty-eight years old whose story was that "everything seemed to go wrong." He had an engaging personality. He was of athletic build and was, as a matter of fact, a professional baseball player. He was a man's man, and it was impossible not to like him. His life was in a pretty bad mess, however. He came of an excellent family and had enjoyed every advantage, but everything he touched seemed to fail. He had now become involved in a bit of dishonesty. He felt that he had plenty of people to blame for his difficulties, and he gave each his full share. As I recall it he even blamed the government a little! The one person he did not blame was himself, but he got around to that later and when he did his troubles began to disappear.

Asked about his religious background, he replied that he had been brought up in the church but religion was a very unimportant matter to him. I pointed out to him that there are two kinds of Christianity. One, "Christianity of form." In this kind of Christianity, one belongs to the church and perhaps does what is referred to as church work. This type of Christianity turns out some splendid people—honorable, morally good, upstanding citizens—likable folk.

Then I told him that there is another form of Christianity which we call "Christianity of Power." In this type, you experience spiritual power in your innermost being. It is like turning on a light in a dark room or throwing a switch of a great motor. It establishes contact with that tremendous force which we call God, and causes spiritual energy to flood your life. In the first type of religion, we have to *try* to be good, but in the latter form one wants to be good so sincerely that one *is* good, and an Inner Power helps us to be good. It is the difference between rowing a boat using your physical energy, and installing a powerful motor in your "craft."

The young man became interested and said: "I'd like to have that kind of religion. How do you get it?" I explained that the way to get it was "to surrender your life to Jesus Christ."

He said, "Do you mean that I must be converted?"

I replied, "You guessed it."

He gave his life to Christ—he really meant it, too—and it "took" with him.

Now, see what happened: A few days later he came around and said, "I see it!"

"You see what?" I asked.

He replied: "I see what's wrong with me. The thing that's wrong with me is *myself*."

"And how did you arrive at that mysterious conclusion?" I asked.

"Well," he said, "after I was converted the other day, something inside of me said: 'Be honest with yourself. You know that's the real reason everything goes wrong.' But," he continued, "they won't go wrong now, because I'm no longer a 'wrong self.' I feel that at last I've found a real power." Subsequent events proved that he had solved his problem.

Of course, there are many people whose problem is not a moral or ethical one. What is their trouble? Often it is that they are thinking a great deal about their troubles and very little about God. That's why everything seems to go wrong. If you start thinking about God and reassure yourself that God is in your life and that He can give you power, then you *have* power over all circumstances.

In *Gone With the Wind,* Margaret Mitchell describes the terrific hardships suffered by the people of the South after the Civil War. One of her characters, in describing a Southern gentleman who had suffered devastating adversity and who broke under it, said: " . . . he could be licked from the inside. I mean to say that what the whole world couldn't do, his own heart could." This simple Southern philosopher continued, "There ain't nothing from the outside can lick any of us."

What Margaret Mitchell says through this character is true. The people who are being beaten by life could win if they would learn to strengthen their hearts. And how do we strengthen our hearts? The answer is by cultivating God. Then we have faith and a strength for every crisis.

Faith is the answer to that deep grief which lies upon the spirit of the unhappy and dissatisfied man. Faith lifts this burden. That is why frequently you hear great congregations sing, "I love to tell the story." As ideals lose their vitality, life sours and grief is formed. As faith wells up, life freshens, grief is driven off. One then becomes so happy he cannot help singing.

SEVEN:

Relief for the Lonely

Relief for the Lonely

SMILEY BLANTON

THE VERY EARLY INFANTILE STATE IS ONE OF COMPLETE self-centeredness. As the child grows, this changes. Some of the love received by him he returns. But the individual must retain a little of that first self-centeredness to be truly happy. Self-depreciation is morbid. It not only prevents us from gaining love but also from giving love to others.

A morbid reaction may be produced by any one of three causes during the childhood period of learning. Sometimes the loved parent does not return love in a wholly satisfactory way. Sometimes the object gives so much that the recipient fears complete domination. Again, the loved object may demand too high a price for love: too much obedience, too much passivity. In any case the child is thrown back on himself when he should not be.

The infant burdened with one or other of those conditions becomes afraid to give his love to others. Such timidity engenders distrust and hostility. Later this may take the form of distrust and hostility toward all the world. Such an individual is likely to find himself without friends, and alone.

It is easy to expect the impossible of life, to believe that life will inevitably bring comradeship and amusement. The loneliness that springs from an incapacity to make friends must be examined.

Mrs. Ruth K. came to the church clinic to talk with the pastor about her inability to find any satisfaction in her religious life. She felt that she must have committed some sin that kept her from the peace that should come through a normal religious life.

To the consulting pyschiatrist she told the following story: She had been brought up in a small New York town. Her home life was not happy. Her earliest memory was of her father and mother quarreling. Her father was self-centered and selfish, and her mother was very critical and nagging. Neither father nor mother would concede anything, and when Ruth was about eight years old they were divorced. She and her mother went to live with her mother's sister, while her brother, a few years older than she, stayed with her father. She rarely saw her father; after she was fifteen, never. She did not even know whether he was alive or dead.

She withdrew into herself, became taciturn. She did well in school and college, but had few friends. After college she found a good position in the city where she and her mother and aunt lived.

At the age of twenty-three she met a charming but somewhat ineffectual man and married him. But "like mother, like daughter." She became overcritical of her husband, of his extravagance when he shopped, of his carelessness, of the lack of initiative which kept him for succeeding in business. Finally he deserted her, giving up his job and going to another part of the country.

She became very restless. Unable to stay in the same place after her experience, she came to New York, where she found another good job. She had been living in New York about ten years when she came to the church clinic.

She did not have a single friend in the city. She would go home after work, cook her own dinner, listen to the radio, and go to bed. She vigorously maintained that the real cause of her loneliness was the difficulty of making friends in New York City. Admittedly, it is difficult for a newcomer to make friends in a large city, but it is also apparent that in the case of an attractive young woman in her early thirties the fault could not lie wholly with the city.

Sympathetic and skillful questioning brought out the following facts: When she first came to New York she had shared an apartment with a college acquaintance, a pleasant and agreeable young woman. But Ruth K. failed to do her share of the housework, did not even fully meet her share of the expenses, and, on the other hand, criticized her roommate's friends without reserve, as well as constantly criticizing her roommate herself by indirection. After six months the roommate terminated the arrangement. After that Ruth K. lived in a woman's hotel.

Men, even the men in the office, she said, were stupid, with puerile interests. Questioning, however, revealed there were several interesting men in the group, and several couples of about her own age and background. There were furthermore the alumnae association of her college, and the social clubs at her church, but she had not bothered about these.

Her critical attitude toward the world, with its attendant loneliness, and even the tragedy of her marriage, sprang from her childhood experiences. When she began to understand this, her attitude changed. Hesitantly she and some of the church groups and later a dramatic society. New interests led to new acquaintances and eventually to friends.

The narcissistic individual who has been forced by circumstances to withdraw his love inside himself inevitably feels a sense of bitterness and anger toward the world.

The father of Miss Eleanor Z. was a successful physician; to everyone he seemed diffident and detached, and even to her, his only child, reserved and strange. Her mother had died when Eleanor was born. Her father did not marry again. His attitude toward her was that of a courteous friend. She was not sure of his love; and she felt that he was avoiding even that emotional commitment. She grew up a lovely and unhappy child.

After graduation from college she specialized in chemistry and became a brilliant research worker. She rose steadily in her field of work, receiving promotion upon promotion. But she became more and more self-centered, withdrew more and more from companionships, and from a healthy mental attitude. She began to have a constant sense of fatigue, of mental strain. Finally she developed a stomach ulcer, then insomnia. She did not neglect her work through this trying period, but became outwardly a hard, bitter, almost surly person. Her assistants feared her, and even those who knew her best thought of her as lacking ordinary human feelings.

One day a woman in the apartment next door, a casual acquaintance, asked her if she did not want to hear a series of lectures on mental hygiene and religion. For lack of anything better to do, she went to the opening one. To her surprise it proved interesting, and she attended the whole series. She then sought an interview at the church clinic.

A few consultations revealed that her bitter manner

and unconscious narcissism were superficial. In reality she had a strong desire for normal human relationships. A remarkable change ensued. She began to attend church again and became a most earnest worker in several of its practical organizations. Her personality changed; her illness passed; she made friends. She had unconsciously been working toward the solution of her problem herself, for without that, the treatment could not have had such remarkable results in so short a time. Even a narcissistic, aggressive personality can be changed through adequate self-understanding.

But not all people accept suggestions or advice. Some of them oppose vigorously whatever is suggested.

John G. came to the church clinic after hearing one of the pastor's radio talks. He was lonely, unhappy, critical, and misunderstood. This critical attitude was valuable in his work: he was the very efficient purchasing agent of a large corporation. But he carried this critical and antagonistic attitude into his personal life. No matter what suggestions were made to him, he always argued violently and refused to accept them.

A business associate would say, "John, come on out to lunch," and although he might really want to go, he would refuse the invitation, alleging there was work left on his desk that had to be done. He naturally had almost no friends, certainly no close ones. His rejection of friendly advances kept everyone at a distance.

But John G. considered that the rest of the world was to blame. People were trying to take advantage of him, they were trying to make him do things against them. But in his heart he really suspected something was wrong and wanted help. The fact that he voluntarily came to the church clinic proved that.

He had been reared in a strict Presbyterian household. His mother, whom he loved with unusual devotion, had inculcated Christian teachings in him. But his excessive devotion to his mother and his mother's devotion to him had begun to threaten his adult emotional life. In his efforts to escape from that he had rejected everyone else's affection as well. So extreme was his revolt that he refused to accept affection from anybody; even the most tentative approach by another person seemed to him like an aggression. Eventually he realized that revolt against the too tight bond with his mother was the basis of his negativism.

Lonely people constantly strive to achieve a greater degree of emotional satisfaction. Sometimes they clutch at casual acquaintances, or strive with an energy worthy of a better cause to make indifferent relationships significant. But while there is room in life for many casual acquaintances, only a very few deep friendships are possible.

The early orderly development of May M.'s love life had been peculiarly frustrated by a kindly but narcissistic mother. May spent her early youth trying to win a warm human response from her mother, but finally gave up. When grown she turned the same full strength of her efforts on her friends. With schoolgirl eagerness she rushed each new acquaintance, and, if they responded at all, rewarded them with long and detailed accounts of her life and disappointments in people. She was constantly putting her friends under obligations to her which they silently resented. They turned down otherwise pleasant minor invitations from her because they had learned that by accepting them they placed themselves under obligation.

May M.'s mother had put her through college, kept house for her, cooked, laundered, and entertained for her without permitting her daughter to assist in any way. But she did demand payment in the form of her daughter's complete dependence. The daughter must confide everything in her, keep nothing back, and allow her to make all decisions.

"Look at all I have done for you," the mother would say repeatedly. Eventually May married in order to escape. She became so bitter and antagonistic to her mother that she would not see her.

Then with the curious necessity that the unconscious mind has for repeating the pattern of the parents' life in our own, she began to assume her mother's very characteristics, and in the end her husband and her friends escaped from her as she had escaped from her mother. In explaining their escape to herself she would give every reason but the right one. But eventually her problem became so pressing that it forced her to develop some insight and eventually to untangle her self-woven web of trouble.

There is still another type of lonely individual who fits in badly in his community. Sometimes he is a superior person trying to get along in an inferior environment. Sometimes he is mismated and trying to make the best of it. Such a person is usually not sure of himself, blames himself and not his environment, and feels that he must change himself.

Emily B. was a very brilliant person. Her father had

entered his own father's hardware business, although his real interest was archaeology. He spent all his spare time reading archaeological works or hunting for arrow heads, pottery, and other remains of Indian culture. He became an expert on the Indian civilization of his region.

Emily's brother liked the hardware business, but she followed her father's scholarly bent. They lived in a suburban community where most of the young people seemed to be interested only in a good time. She had very few friends; most of the men thought she was "highbrow." She liked to walk and dance, but what she wanted most was to have friends with whom she could discuss the things that interested her. She was always having to suppress a desire to talk about such things as E. E. Cummings's work, or the stream-of-consciousness writing of Gertrude Stein, or James Joyce. But there was not a single young person in her community who cared for that kind of thing. She began to fear that perhaps she was queer, and that her loneliness might make her queerer.

It took her some time to realize that she was quite normal and merely misplaced. When she learned to look elsewhere than in her own community for people of like tastes, her problem was solved.

Loneliness is too much taken for granted. Some loneliness is inevitable. But before it is accepted as such its possible unconscious source should be examined.

Relief for the Lonely

NORMAN VINCENT PEALE

IN COMPILING A LIST OF THE WORLD'S GREATEST NOVELS, an eminent professor of literature gave first place to that thrilling old classic, *Robinson Crusoe*. He justified his action on the grounds that not only is it the first English novel, but it is wrought, as every great novel must be, out of a fundamental fact of human experience. A great novel must deal with a profound truth about life. This *Robinson Crusoe* does with surpassing genius.

It portrays a man fallen upon a most terrible fate—that of loneliness. The highlight of the book which stirs every reader is the chapter in which the cure for that loneliness is found. Every day Crusoe comes to his lookout point, where he has rigged up a cloth at the top of a pole. He stands gazing across the sea, hands shading his eyes, searching for white sails against the empty horizon.

Standing there in his tatters, skin bronzed, hair long and unkempt, the beach grass waving at his feet, utterly alone, he is a tragic figure. He longs for the touch of a a human hand, the sound of a human voice, and the friendly light of a human face. His solitary vigil once again unrewarded, he turns to go but stops short in wild surprise, for before him in the sands of his supposedly desert island is an unmistakable human footprint, not his own.

In a manner usually less dramatic but no less poignant,

every man in the long voyage of the years is likely to find himself, like Crusoe, upon some lonely island of the spirit. Indeed, there is a fundamental loneliness which haunts all who think deeply upon human experience. Man, at birth, enters this world alone from out the vast silences. Here he comes to be closely bound to others by strong ties of love and friendship. Yet in him remains a mystic homesickness, as if he does not really belong here but is, as an old hymn says, "A pilgrim and a stranger." Literature, art, and music, man's means of expressing himself, give utterance to this cosmic loneliness.

Sculptors, painters, and writers have given us the thought that we are not detached spirits, each living his allotted three score and ten, but are elements in the ceaseless flow of eternity. Sir James Jeans, the eminent scientist, touched on the same thought when he said, "It may be that each individual consciousness is a brain cell in a universal mind." According to Jeans, we do not live as distinct entities for a limited moment of time but tarry on earth during what is called human life, passing on finally, not to extinction as though our purpose were accomplished, but to further functioning in other capacities in the never-ending process of a cosmic mind of which each of us is a constituent part. It is a noble thought and may explain that vague loneliness which the thoughtful man feels now and then, as though somehow he did not really belong here but felt the pull of some mystic homeland ever drawing his restless feet toward it.

Doctor Blanton has presented several concrete studies in personal experience, each illustrating how an abnormal loneliness adversely affects personal happiness. I now wish to show not only how religion effectively deals with the cosmic loneliness described above, but also how it acts

curatively on the loneliness brought us from time to time
by the experiences and circumstances of our lives.

My experience as a pastor has clearly shown me that a
genuine Christian is never a victim of loneliness. Mark
you, I said a *genuine* Christian, and that of course, does
not mean everyone who goes to church and glibly recites
the creeds. A genuine Christian is one who sincerely tries
to live in the spirit of Christ, has a simple trust and who
has mastered the workable techniques of faith. This type
of Christian has a friendly and sympathetic attitude
toward all men. He is kindly in his relationships, and
possesses a generous spirit, which is well able to lift him
above everyday frictions. Moreover, he has learned to
cope with shyness and oversensitiveness, because he has
conquered the ego-centeredness which causes them. The
Christ-like spirit that actuates him makes him too big for
that carping pettiness which destroys friendships, leaving
one forsaken and alone.

I have noticed also, that the genuine Christian, though
he may be compelled by circumstances to be much alone,
is not lonely, for he has inner resources to draw upon and
consequently always finds himself in good company. As a
man playing solitaire whiles away the lonely hours
pleasantly because he enjoys his own game, so the man
with worthwhile thoughts in his mind can play life's game
alone because he is interesting even to himself. The important factor is what is in one's mind.

William Lyon Phelps, in his *Autobiography,* tells us
that the happiest man is he who thinks the most interesting thoughts. Many people are lonely because they live
in empty houses, considering the sparse furnishing of their
minds. Marcus Aurelius wisely observed that "Man must
be arched and buttressed from within, else the temple

wavers to the dust." He also tells us that "The happiness of our life depends upon the quality of our thoughts." Edna St. Vincent Millay warns us,

> "And he whose soul is flat—the sky
> Will cave in on him by and by."*

Many people never read anything worth while; some never read at all, save the newspaper headlines. The extent of this indifference to good reading is evidenced by the astonishing prevalence of picture publications. The person who stocks his mind with great thoughts lays up treasures not only in heaven but here and now, within himself, treasures and resources upon which he may live happily, finding himself interesting enough to make loneliness impossible.

The Christian's weapon against loneliness is his faith. By means of this faith he has the ability to deal successfully with loneliness in any of its forms. His faith, for one thing, takes him to church. The church is the supreme fellowship of all the agencies which bring men together. Our age, conscious of the need of man for fellowship, has established clubs where it is ruled that men must hail each other by their first names and slap each other familiarly on the back. This is to compensate for the loss of the old-time neighborliness which prevailed when American communities were smaller and life less hurried. All of this is well enough, but a fellowship is needed that goes deeper into man's experience.

Only the church can provide this deeper fellowship. A church congregation gathered for the worship of God is

---

* *Renascence*, Harper & Brothers, New York.

different from any other audience. In the church is that intangible bond which binds together common seekers after God. Men may come into a church in a great city having no personal acquaintance with anyone in the congregation, but if the church be true to the spirit of Christianity, the sense of strangeness falls away under the consciousness that all are brothers in their relationship to a common God. They sense that here is God's house, the true home of the soul, that here is brotherhood because here is fatherhood—God's Fatherhood.

When a man comes into such a true church carrying in his mind the old human struggle against discouragement, sorrow, temptation and sin, he looks about him and knows that every other honest worshipper is laying before God identical problems. A common feeling respecting the deepest things of life forges an unspoken fellowship and understanding in which the lonely person finds satisfaction.

Some churches, to be sure, do not offer this atmosphere; they have grow cold and formal and stereotyped. Where vital religion exists, however, the church becomes the deepest fellowship of all; the place where men's experience with God is shared. A salesman from a Western city tells me that he is helped by attending our mid-week service on his frequent trips to New York. Though he is not acquainted with any of the people present, he finds courage and strength by looking around at faces in which, he says, he sees the light of faith and goodness. This fellowship, he declares, lifts his loneliness and aids him in his business responsibilities of the next day.

The fellowship of the church dissipates loneliness and creates a unity of spirit among those who go together into high places. It is the bond between men who enter into the comradeship of a great adventure. It is the understanding of men who have felt the same urge, experienced God's presence together, and who talk the same language of the spirit.

Some years ago in my congregation was a wonderful old man, one of the finest spirits I have known. He was a successful business man. He knew God personally if ever a human being did, and while officially I was his pastor our roles were really reversed. Whenever I needed new inspiration and courage, I always talked to him and never came away without a tremendous uplift. He gave good advice; but more than that, he brought you near to God and sent you away eager and well able to attack your problems vigorously.

I well recall my last visit with him. I drove late one autumn evening to his summer home, where he lingered late in the season. I passed over the hills, down into a valley along a little babbling stream, across a white bridge, and there was the century-old farmhouse where he had been born and where he was to die. I walked up on the porch and rapped on the door. The old man opened it and peered out into the night, holding an old-fashioned kerosene lamp above his head. With a smile and word of welcome he ushered me into the old-style parlor. With trembling fingers he turned up the light and we talked. Before time to go he took up an old Bible, much worn, held it in his aged hands and read in gentle tones from the sacred volume. Then we knelt in prayer as men had been kneeling in that American farmhouse for a hundred years; in the old-fashioned sitting room in the mellow light of the lamp. I looked on his face as he prayed, a fine face seamed and wrinkled with years, but also the face of a little child talking to his father.

It was no miniature prayer of one who had little to say. It was a man-sized prayer of a great old Christian talking to his God, with whom he would rather speak than with anyone on earth. My knees became painfully conscious of the thinly carpeted floor, but as we climbed to "high places" in that prayer, my weariness left me, earth seemed to fade away and God drew near. Americans have knelt in such parlors throughout all our history, and it was prayers offered by strong men like this friend of mine that helped to make this Republic. It was communion like this that made men see and feel the greatness, the romance, and the spirituality of life.

As I left the valley and climbed into the hills I looked back and saw the little house with the lamp in the window, and the verse of an old hymn ran through my mind:

"Blest be the tie that binds
Our hearts in Christian love;
The fellowship of kindred minds
Is like to that above."

Fellowship like this is found only in the Church. It was entry into such fellowship that took away the loneliness of the people mentioned by Doctor Blanton in his section of this chapter. They found in the Church not only the power which gives meaning and joy to life, but the alchemy of Christian fellowship as well. They participated in this fellowship, not alone in church worship but through the various organizations of the Church which have been created for service and for the enjoyment and enrichment of social contact under auspices which guarantee worthwhile and interesting people.

I regret that I do not have space enough to relate some

of the stories of modern young people who came to New York City from every section of America, who, made lonely by difficult circumstances, found what amounts to new life in our Youth Groups. They have come, by one avenue or another, into our church clinic, lonely and discouraged, and later I have seen them with several hundred other young people in our Thursday-night group—Young Adult Group—or other young people's organizations, overcoming the abnormal withdrawal into themselves which was making them victims of loneliness and thereby causing them to fail. Our men's clubs and women's organizations and our business women's clubs contain many a happy soul who has finally discovered in the wholesome, friendly and spiritual atmosphere of the Church that genuine fellowship with fine people which makes life worth living.

Our church has a motto which has done as much good as many sermons and more than not a few—"Where Old-Fashioned Friendliness Still Survives." Churches at the heart of great cities, or, for that matter, anywhere else, can do vast good by emphasizing that human interest and cordiality is assuredly related to real religion, which helps to cure modern people of maladies of personality brought on by the ingrown life so common in our time.

Faith is the answer to the problem of loneliness. As a pastor I have seen evidence of this assertion too many times to have any doubt about it. Consider the loneliness of bereavement. A loved one has been taken by death. For awhile the reaction is one of acute lonesomeness, the agony of separation. The bereaved one misses the object of his love with all the pain and grief. The danger is that the grief may become abnormal through the withdrawal of one's love into oneself and result in bitterness toward an unkind world. There are thousands of people today whose lives are disintegrating because they have not developed enough faith to cope with the sorrow that breaks down their personalities.

The man of faith, although he suffers the pain of bereavement, at the same time believes that "all things work together for good to them that love God." He believes that the soul is immortal and that God is a Being with absolute love in his heart. He turns to God for comfort, and God does not disappoint him. If his faith is strong enough, it makes his consciousness of the Divine compassion and protection so complete that loneliness vanishes and a sense of companionship takes its place.

I had always preached about the power of faith in times of sorrow; then one day very suddenly my mother died while still a comparatively young woman. It was the first personal bereavement I had ever known and I wondered if my faith would meet the test. I found when I was forced to depend on it that it did work. I did what I had often advised others to do. I trusted God completely and asked for and took the comfort He offered. I had been with my mother in her home in upstate New York until midnight the night before she died and had left her to take a night train. My heart had rejoiced, for she seemed to be recovering from her illness.

Fifteen minutes after I arrived in New York City the next morning, I received the heartbreaking news that she had just passed away. I fought the battle of shock and grief in my study at the church. As I stood by my desk, I had the most unusual experience in my life. My hands happened to be resting upon a Bible and I was staring out on the street when suddenly I seemed to feel two cupped hands rest lightly on my head, softer than eiderdown and only for a fleeting moment but unmistakable and definite. It was as if my mother, knowing my need, was attempting to draw near from another world to comfort me. I recognize all the facile objections which may be urged against the reality of this experience, and my reason dealt thoroughly with the question of whether the experience was real, but the sense of my mother's presence, even to the light touch upon the head, has, for me at least, the quality of certainty.

Nor was this all. Upon arrival next day at the family home I related my experience to my father, a man of exceedingly factual and scientific mind. I told him about it with great diffidence because I knew the skeptical slant of his mind regarding such phenomena. To my surprise, he replied that a similar experience had come to him about two hours after my mother's death. He told me that he went out into the garden to a summerhouse and sat stunned and heartbroken. He felt that an irresistible force had swept her away, that she was gone forever. He put his head on his arms on the table and burst into sobs. Suddenly he seemed to feel the presence of my mother as if she stood by his side. The feeling was so real that he looked up almost as if he expected to see her there. He sensed in her a warmth, a glow of ecstasy that was different and beyond anything in this world—a supernatural joy. Then it seemed that she placed her hand ever so lightly on his forehead, her arm seemed to encircle his neck, and he felt rather than heard her speak his name with all the familiar intonations of her voice. She gave him the unmistakable impression that she was perfectly happy, filled with a radiant joy beyond anything she had known in this world.

I am not competent to analyze scientifically these inti-

mate and tender incidents, nor would I care to examine
them in that way. I mention them here because of the viv-
idness with which they came to two quite different minds
as the result of a combination of need and faith. They
brought profound comfort and soothed our great loneliness, first by convincing us that our loved one was in a
place of great peace and far happier there than in this
world of pain, and second, through the mystic assurance
of her nearness. I cannot answer why all men of faith do
not have similar experiences, but when I have told this
story, many very rational and unemotional people have
testified that when they have adventured far into faith,
phenomena similar in nature, though different in form,
have entered into their lives with healing comfort to as-
suage the loneliness of bereavement.

Many men and women are also lonely because, as was
said in the first part of this chapter, some inward disorganization of personality unconsciously makes them repel
others. Here again is the answer, for faith helps to untangle the mental processes and corrects this disorganization.
One of the first things that faith does is to make a man
honest with himself. This is as necessary for the cure of
maladies of the personality as it is for physical ones.
When you are ill and go to a physician, you do not hide
from him anything necessary to proper diagnosis and
treatment. He must have all the facts, honestly laid before
him. When we deal with the mind, we must remember
that it has a strong tendency to rationalize or excuse its
own faults. It seems to invent reasons why we are what
we are rather than to face our faults frankly and examine
and seek to correct them. Faith puts the light of reason on
the problem. Then the individual becomes able to receive
the healing power of God.

I know a man, for example, who felt that everybody was talking about him and criticizing him. He believed that no one liked him. He wanted the respect and affection of his associates. He had a genuine desire to be of service, proved by the fact that he belonged to a number of organizations and fraternal orders and was a member of the church. In each of these organizations he had gradually become an officer. He won these posts because he was a hard-working member, and in one or two instances employed a little politics. But he was unhappy because he realized that he did not really share in the fellowship which was apparent all around him. He wasn't "one of the crowd." This wounded him deeply, and one day he asked himself frankly the reason for this. Then he came to see me, believing that in the confidential clinic at our church, he could talk about himself and the problem freely and without restraint, and receive the guidance he sought.

As we talked he began to see that the reason he felt people were criticizing him was because he was critical of everybody else; that the reason people did not like him was because they were instinctively aware that he did not like them; that the cause of his loneliness was because he was repelling people. He saw that his entire attitude was basically unkind and that his mind instantly began to pick flaws in people he met, that he could not allow anyone to hold an opinion different from his own, and that he had a tendency to correct everybody according to his own standards.

He put the X-ray of an honest, thoroughgoing analysis on himself. It was difficult for him to admit that the people he had been criticizing were not so bad after all, and that he himself was at fault. But he came to see clearly that his trouble with people was not due to them, but was, rather, a projection of his own wrong attitudes. The instant he became aware of this, the healing process began. Today he is a happy, popular, worthwhile individual, and his loneliness is entirely cured.

Loneliness lurks in the shadows of adversity. By a curious psychological osmosis, these shadows of adverse circumstance seep into the inward life. Often, especially in times of dark personal vicissitudes, such shadows develop morbid loneliness. The sure antidote is a warmhearted radiant faith which can shed light into the darkness. Motor-car manufacturers have not yet perfected a truly efficient light to penetrate heavy fog, but religion provides such a light for the individual lost and lonely in the fog of pain and suffering.

An old Russian proverb says, "The hammer shatters glass, but forges steel." Some people are like glass—the hammer of circumstance breaks them in pieces. Other people are like steel—the hammer strikes and, instead of breaking them, forges them into new forms of strength and beauty. Christianity puts the steel-like element in people, so that they do not break under the hammer blows of circumstance. The resiliency is given them by their faith.

I recently read *I Begin Again,* an inspiring book by a blind woman, Alice Bretz. It is an heroic story out of real life, the autobiography of a radiant soul. She had loved the subtle lights and shadings of this beautiful world. She had a rare sense of appreciation. She had loved to see dawn come, lifting a curtain from the hills—the ancient mystery of returning day. She had loved to see the sunlight sifting down through the leaves, splashing onto a well-kept lawn in the summertime. She had liked to see the sunlight speckling the cool earth along a trout stream on a lazy summer afternoon. She had liked to see the sun falling behind the hills at the close of day, sending a last long shaft of light to spotlight the flowers in her garden. She was thrilled by the sight of silvery moonlight streaming down on rippling waters on a starry night. Then suddenly a haze came over her eyes and darkness fell, and she went to the hospital.

She thought it was only temporary blindness. Spring came and she wanted to get back to her home—her farm. She eagerly anticipated the delight of her apple trees in blossom filling the atmosphere with fragrance and loveliness. Then the doctor came to her. He was a blunt fellow and said, "I am sorry to tell you that you are blind. You will never see again."

She said quietly, "Doctor, it must have been very hard for you to say that."

Then as she lay in the darkness, she felt that some terror was on her breast ready to pounce upon her. She recoiled in horror; it was the terror of the dark.

Then came a clergyman to her side, and he put his hand on her head and said, "God has laid his cross on you, my child." And he went away.

As she lay there she could feel this great, heavy cross crushing her. She was weighted down by it. She began to think of the cross. She remembered the church where as a girl she had been confirmed, where she worshipped. She recalled how the church looked on a Sunday morning with the brilliant sunlight streaming through the art-glass windows. She could see, in memory, the sunlight falling upon the gold of the cross, causing it to gleam as it passed in the processional. She could hear the hymn that they always sang when they came in bearing the cross:

> "Onward, Christian soldiers!
> Marching as to war,
> With the cross of Jesus
> Going on before."

The truth then came flashing in upon her darkened mind. The cross always goes on before. It is not something to crush us. The cross is the symbol of victory, of triumph!

"Though I must be blind the rest of my days," she cried, "I will turn my cross into victory and let it lead me as a singing soul. I will not be defeated! I will triumph through Christ who gives me strength."

Any loneliness in this life can be dissipated by the power of faith.

EIGHT:
Love and Marriage

Love and Marriage

SMILEY BLANTON

ONE OF THE DIFFICULTIES IN DISCUSSING LOVE IS THAT the psychiatrist uses the word with a much wider meaning than the popular one. Therefore is is necessary to explain his use of it. "Love" is feeling which tends to draw us toward a person or object—and "hate" is any feeling that tends to pull us away from such an object. Obviously, the word "love" so used includes emotions of lesser intensity not involved in its popular use. "Love," for instance, includes "liking" and even "tolerance of."

Love is usually thought of as a violent emotion and, more than that, as having a special quality of its own, as being different from "liking" in quality as well as in degree. This violent emotion is popularly identified with the "being-in-love" of adult men and women or the love of parent and child for each other. But it has other values, such as in "love of the land," and "love of freedom."

The psychiatrist holds that in the final analysis all of these loves—of wife, husband, parent, child, brothers, sisters, country, freedom, and even of pets, books, food—are of one great piece.

The love that accompanies the impulse to reproduce is sexualized. The rest—the greater part by far—is devoid of erotic sensation.

It is necessary that the reader accept, at least tentatively, the psychiatrist's definition of love, so that he may understand this chapter clearly.

All activity is accompanied by sensation either pleasant or unpleasant. The child is in a process of learning to avoid the unpleasant activities and to seek the pleasant ones. Strongly pleasurable sensations go with eating, being gently handled by those he loves, being bathed, caressed, et cetera.

Normally as the child grows older his love centers more and more on people and things and less and less on processes and sensations connected with his own body. But if, through the accident of rearing, he has insufficient normal outlet for his developing love for people, this developing love may turn inward on his body processes and sensations and give them a strongly erotic tinge. When he continues to feel pleasurable emotions about physical processes which should become free of them, there develops an undue sense of guilt and a resulting fear of all pleasurable emotions of whatever kind.

Out of this condition arises an erroneous concept of love as being of two kinds, one pure, the other impure; the one holy, the other guilty; or perhaps one of the spirit and the other of the body. Of course the reproductive impulse is strong, and although neither impure nor guilty, must be disciplined and controlled. This is fully recognized both by highly civilized and by primitive men. But the false distinctions between "pure" and "sexual" love may easily give rise to serious maladjustment in marriage. It may prevent a healthy satisfaction in both the physical and the spiritual life by driving a wedge between them. A concept of love as divided into "clean" and "unclean" is one of the major factors in causing unhappiness in marriage, and even when it does not break up the marriage, it causes so much friction and tension that children of that marriage often develop serious emotional difficulties.

If the whole love relationship in marriage is a sacrament, with the method of reproduction ordained by the Creator, it cannot, at the proper time and in the proper place, be unclean, repulsive, or sinful.

Mrs. Dona R. came to the church clinic because of her desperate marital unhappiness. Her husband was brilliant and earnest but had a very inflexible personality. She had been aware of his inflexibility, but she felt their marriage would nevertheless be happy. After they married he told her he thought they ought not to have sexual relations until they wanted a child, and they had agreed they could not afford a child for two years. To live as man and wife meantime, he said, would be merely "pandering to the flesh."

This disturbed Mrs. R. very much because she did not share his feeling that physical love was unclean. Much against her will she agreed because she felt it her duty as a loyal wife.

After a year they began to live together as man and wife and after that their first child was born. Then they refrained for two years until they wanted another child.

When Mrs. R. came to the church clinic the minister and psychiatrist working together easily reassured her that there was no justification for her husband's behavior either in the teachings of the Church or in the Bible. They finally succeeded in modifying the husband's belief, although it was far from easy, for his difficulty lay very deep.

This adult feeling of impurity concerning the physical side of love very often arises in earliest childhood when the child is made ashamed of his body by unwise scoldings or punishments for some childish behavior, especially of finding pleasure by touching his own body. This impurity feeling not only affects the whole physical side of love, but sometimes gives rise to such strong feelings of guilt and shame as to produce serious emotional maladjustments throughout life.

Some time ago a young man of eighteen played football on the high-school team, and after one of the plays lay helpless on the ground. He said that his back was hurt and that he could not move his legs. His father hurried him to a hospital in New York City. The doctors made a very careful examination but found no physical injury to account for the apparently complete paralysis of his legs.

The boy was in a highly emotional state. He was sure he was going to die and wanted to make his peace with God. He asked for a minister. The pastor hurried from the church clinic to his bedside and after some conversation realized from the boy's profound anxiety that he probably had some special burden on his mind.

He finally confessed to the minister that he believed his trouble was due to a secret sin—self-abuse. He said he had tried to resist it ever since the age of ten, when his father told him if he didn't stop it, his backbone would be eaten away. He tried hard to stop the habit but once in a while it recurred. When in the midst of the football game he suddenly felt the wrench in his back, he believed that his sins had caught up with him, that he must have "committed the unforgivable sin," and that now he would surely die.

The pastor first learned from the physicians that the boy was physically unhurt and that his condition was due to what is known as an hysterical paralysis. He then assured him that his act was certainly not unforgivable and that it was an unfortunate habit that had persisted. Finally he suggested that the boy see the consultant psychiatrist of the church clinic. The boy accepted this suggestion and the minister and the psychiatrist working together succeeded in ridding him of his fear, eliminating his hysterical paralysis, and setting his mind straight about the feeling of guilt.

Not many cases are as clear cut as this, but our experience is that a great many adults suffer from a morbid sense of guilt concerning things which are merely unfortunate habits carried over from childhood, but which they have misinterpreted as something unforgivable.

The pastor one day received the following letter from a young man who lives some distance from New York:

"I have read your book, The Art of Living, and in it the many instances where you have helped sin-sick souls. Could you help me, because I am desperate? I am twenty-one years old and I have been guilty of something that stops the flow of normal power through my mind. I have not been able to rid myself of this terrible habit, and I am afraid my soul is lost. I feel that life is not worth living. I have prayed and I cannot seem to get close to God, but I am praying that this letter will bring me help. There is no one here I can tell this to, neither my pastor, my doctor, nor my parents."

The man's extreme reaction to what the whole race has experienced (the young child's tendency to caress himself) shows the danger of punishing or scolding a young child about it.

Another problem having its origin in childhood and which is more frequent than many suppose is that of an undue degree of love for persons of the same sex. This condition gives rise to anxieties and depressions which may disrupt the person's life. As a child he loved both his father and his mother. That is a necessary pattern in group living. It is normal to love people both of the same sex and of the opposite sex. But a balance must be kept between them. If a young man likes so much being with young men that he doesn't care ever to go with girls, or if a girl is so interested in girls that she does not care to have men friends, there is obviously a lack of balance in his or her love life.

It is one of the functions of psychiatry to help such people to understand themselves and to reorganize their lives on a saner basis. But not much can be accomplished if they think of the tendency as such a horribly guilty thing that they are damned forever. Such an impulse in young people is obviously due to an early, childish relationship for which they are not to blame. An impulse for which they are not to blame can usually be eliminated through their coming to an understanding of the deeper, unconscious motives developed in childhood.

How strong the feeling of guilt may be is evident from a letter the pastor received some time ago:

"Forgive me for troubling you with my problem, but I am in such an unhappy, unbalanced emotional state that I must speak to someone. I have made a good record. I am respected by my friends, and have even been given a position in our church, but my life is a despicable and horrible lie.

"Two years ago I read a book that revealed to me the unfortunate tendency that I have. The author of the book used these words: 'God in his infinite wisdom has seen fit to create an intermediate sex, who find their love satisfaction in the same sex rather than in the opposite sex,' and the book goes on to say that there is no cure for this condition. How can God want people such as I to live?

"Will you please help!"

This young man was deeply depressed and badly needed help. The first thing to do was to assure him that his author's view of the problem was neither truly scientific nor sensible. The book was a wholly outdated one, and he was assured that the author's pronouncement could well be dismissed from his mind.

In his case too there was the unwholesome division between physical and spiritual love. He felt that physical love was too impure and too unclean, that women were too far above him, too pure, that marriage would be impossible.

The origin of his impulses was explained to him, and since he lived in another city he was referred to his own pastor and to a psychiatrist, who helped him modify his morbid sense of guilt and so to moderate his impulses. take vows of chastity, and live affective and happy lives.

A great many conferences are always necessary to change this condition, for it must be done with unhurried patience.

One of the most important problems to young people is the control of the sexual urge until they can be suitably and happily married. This problem is one of the really difficult ones that face our civilization. It requires the best efforts of the home, the church, the school, the parents, the pastor, the teacher, and the physician.

The sexual urge varies widely in various people and so cannot be judged superficially. In some it is more insistent than in others. Some people easily go through their whole lives both chaste and healthy. Some join religious orders, take vows of chastity, and live effective and happy lives.

Others, outside of religious orders, choose for various reasons not to marry, and to remain chaste. To live this way they pay a certain price, it is true, but for some people that price is not too high.

But it is also true that in present-day civilization where marriages often do not occur until the late twenties or later, physical continence is difficult.

What should be said to young people who face the question of whether to hold in check or how much to hold in check this imperious impulse for years and years, while they go through high school, through college, through professional school, and then make a position for themselves so that they can marry and found a home? It is not the function of physician or the psychiatrist to act as a judge in this matter.

As for the psychiatrist, there are certain things he can say which may help. When young unmarried people ask, "Isn't it all right for me to satisfy this sexual urge?" the psychiatrist can only reply that they should first consider certain facts. First—at least in the case of young women —is the danger of injury to reputation which may seriously interfere with their life work; second, sexual relations indulged in on a purely physical plane give little pleasure. Such relations leave only feelings of frustration and vague disgust.

The young people may reply, "If, then, we must not

express our sexual urge until we find a satisfactory partner, what can we do to control the desire?" The answer is, "The best way is through sublimation; that is, to find an otherwise happy, rich social relationship with the opposite sex without physical relations." The home, the church, and the school should find more and better ways in which young people can sublimate this dominant urge through social contact and stimulating work and play together. Hikes, parties, dances, clubs in which the members of both sexes meet for political and social study are needed in greater number and more interesting quality.

A true marriage has a wholesome physical basis, but involved with this are certain necessary spiritual and emotional values. A temporary, secret, furtive, extramarital relationship in which is faced the danger of social disapproval and even disgrace, a relationship in which the emotional and spiritual values play no part, is virtually unable to give any satisfaction. The fear and guilt that usually accompany any such relationship generally outweigh the physical satisfaction.

If, however, young people are driven by this urge to have sex relations before marriage, it is best that the matter should be dealt with sympathetically.

Love itself, in the wider meaning, is a fundamental necessity of life. Sigmund Freud has said: ". . . we must . . . love in order that we may not fall ill, and must fall ill, if, in consequence of frustration, we cannot love."*

The fear of love is very well exemplified by the tragic life of John Ruskin, the man who fought with his pen for social justice in the nineteenth century.

---

* *Collected Papers*, Vol. IV, p. 42.

He was born in 1819, the only child of elderly Scottish parents. His parents had worked hard for their place in the world and had high ambitions for him. They treated him with great severity and at the same time enveloped him in an entangling love. He was early refused toys of any kind. When he reached the age of six he was allowed a ball, a cart and some wooden blocks. He was whipped when he fell downstairs, and he was once allowed to burn his hand on a hot urn in order to teach him how deceitful the world is. The pathos of his early years is told by Ruskin himself:

"I could pass my days contentedly in tracing the squares and comparing the colors of my carpet—examining the knots in the wood of the floor, or counting the bricks in the opposite houses. . . ."*

His aunt gave him a Punch and Judy show, but his mother quietly told him that he ought not to have it, and he never saw it again.

From the time that he could read at the age of four or five, he had to spend hours sitting at his mother's knee alternating with her in reading verses of the Bible:

"And Abijah stood up upon Mount Zemaraim, which is in Mount Ephraim, and said, Hear me, thou Jeroboam, and all Israel."

What was the result of his parents' attitude toward him on Ruskin's attitude toward God? He says:

"My parents were—in a sort—visible powers of nature to me, no more loved than the sun and the moon; . . . still less did I love God . . . but . . . found . . . His service disagreeable. . . ."

* Amable Williams-Ellis, *The Exquisite Tragedy: An Intimate Life of John Ruskin*, Doubleday, Doran, New York, 1929, p. 16.

Of companionship and love he says:

"When affection did come, it came with violence utterly rampant and unmanageable, at least by me, who never before had anything to manage."

When Ruskin grew up and went abroad, he fell in love with a French girl. His parents were scandalized, brought him home, and soon afterward married him to Miss Euphemia Chalmers Gray who they thought would be a suitable wife for him. But Ruskin was so afraid of love that he was never able to consummate the marriage, and so some years later it was annulled and she married John Everett Millais, the painter, and raised a large family.

Ruskin spent most of his energy warring against the social injustice that was about him. But he could see no gaiety or lightness in anything. One day when he was with Doctor Jowett, the Master of Balliol College, Jowett suddenly broke into a hearty ringing laugh. Ruskin sprang up and grasped his hands. "Master," he said, "how delighted I am to hear you! I wish I could laugh like that!"

Later Ruskin wrote to his father:

"Men ought to be severely disciplined and exercised in the sternest way in daily life—they should learn to lie on stone beds and eat black soup, but they should never have their hearts broken. . . . The two terrific mistakes which Mamma and you involuntarily fell into were the exact reverse of this in both ways—you fed me effeminately and luxuriously to that extent that I actually now could not travel in rough countries without taking a cook with me!—But you thwarted me in all the earnest fire of passion and life."

At the age of about fifty-five Ruskin fell in love with Rose La Touche, sixteen, whom he was tutoring. When he told her parents of his feeling for her, they forbade

him to see her again. A year or so later Rose died. Sometime after that Ruskin had a mental breakdown.

Love repressed does strange things. It sometimes dis-
rupts lives. Sometimes the tragedies are of the person's
own making, but sometimes they have been made for him
by well-meaning but unthinking parents who in trying to
make him conform to unsuitable ideals have stultified his
life and reduced his efforts at living to a few futile ges-
tures.

Love and Marriage

NORMAN VINCENT PEALE

OVER A PERIOD OF YEARS, AS MINISTER OF A FIFTH
Avenue church in New York City, it has been my pleasant
duty to marry several thousand couples. During this
period, I have been consulted as a pastor by scores of
couples regarding marital problems, and having had this
experience one acquires a few ideas and some true insight
concerning happiness in marriage.

I am convinced that marriage between intelligent and
sincere persons can be happy and successful. If there is
real, honorable, spiritual love and a sincere desire to
make a union succeed, it can be done. It cannot be over-
stressed that the important factor in happy marriage is the
determination to make it work.

This means that both parties must be psychologically
inclined toward a positive attitude in their marriage. Their
mental objective must be success, not failure. They must
think in terms of success, and we know if the mind thinks
success intensely enough and long enough, it tends to produce success. The possibility of failure must not be given
"mind room."

When a sincere couple will take seriously the words,
"until death us do part," and never even remotely enter-
tain the thought that if their union does not work they can
get out of it, their marriage *must* work because they want

it to work, and because they repudiate in their souls any other alternative.

In any relationship of this life you can get along with the other person if you really want to and if you will keep at it long and earnestly enough. One of the finest intellectual thrills of life is that of studying a personality you love and interweaving your own with it to make that beautiful unity wherein "They twain shall be one flesh."

That is the kind of marriage which is said to be made in heaven, and no doubt the impulse did come from there, but the actual construction work is done on earth by a real man and a real woman who have the will and the faith. I do not mean to infer that happy and successful marriage is always easy. It is sometimes very difficult, but I do say it is not impossible between honest and intelligent people. Should complicated problems arise, I would suggest that to faith should be added the insight and skill in personality adjustments of a spiritually-minded psychiatrist. It may also be wise to seek the advice of a physician of similar point of view. The psychiatrist, the medical man, and the pastor often effectively cooperate in solving marital problems when they become complicated.

There is another ingredient besides will and effort essential to the successful marriage. That is the element our parents took into their new home, and which helped to keep them loving one another through forty or fifty years. I refer to religion. The wisest book ever written and the most expert in human problems says: "Except the Lord build the house, they labor in vain that build it."

In the old-fashioned home of a generation ago, a Bible invariably lay on the center table, and it was read too. Grace was said at meals, prayers were offered at bedtime, and the entire family went to church on Sunday. The one place the parents did not go to was Reno. They built their home around God and religious idealism. That spirit produced character and normal, wholesome minds. It made people proficient in the fine art of personal adjustments.

These religious American people were not plaster saints, but undoubtedly there were some failures in marriage, but by and large their homes demonstrated the secret of happy married life, which the many irreligious homes of today must rediscover not only for the sake of personal happiness but for the future well-being of the country.

I believe any man and wife can make a success of their marriage if they enter upon it in a spiritual attitude. I advise couples to pray together the first night of their marriage and every night thereafter. I know scores of present-day young couples who say grace at meals and many more who frequently read together from the Bible. These marriages do not break. They are cemented by the greatest Power in the world—faith in God.

I have seen many failing marriages saved and permanently restored when both or even one of the partners was willing to bring religion into the situation.

A young woman came to me and said that "she and her husband had reached the breaking point." Misunderstanding had grown to enormous proportions and frequent differences had developed into hateful and bitter quarreling. She was about ready for the divorce court, she said, and I gathered he felt the same way. But she had a sensitive conscience about divorce, and besides, down deep, as it later appeared, she still loved her husband and, of course, wanted to save their marriage.

"Have you, as a minister, any suggestions to make?" she asked.

"Yes, I have a suggestion," I replied. "I have known it to work in other cases like yours and, in fact, it will work in any situation if it is faithfully tried."

"What is it?" she demanded, half skeptical, half hopeful.

"Pray with your husband," I said. "Go home and get him to pray with you."

"Oh," she answered, her face fallen with disappointment, "I couldn't do that. He would make fun of me. We did pray together every night when we were first married, but we gave that up long ago."

"It will work," I replied. "I want you to promise that you will pray with him tonight."

She did not say she would, but next day she was back again as radiant a young woman as I ever saw. She fairly bubbled over with excitement and joy as she told me how she had struggled all evening for courage to make the suggestion to her husband, who was deeply entrenched in his newspaper.

Finally she went over to him and said, "Jim, we can't seem to get together any other way, and all our arguments don't get us anywhere, and, Jim, in spite of everything, I really love you. Will you do one thing for me—will you—will you pray with me like we used to?"

She said he looked at her rather strangely.

"And then what do you think he said?" she asked. "He said, 'I thought of that a couple of times myself, but I didn't have the nerve to suggest it.'

"Why," she cried, "it was wonderful, unbelievable; we got down on our knees as we did when we were first married, and we talked to God like a couple of children, and all the trouble seemed to melt away all at once."

"Keep it up," I urged her, "and you will hold that refound happiness."

"It's a miracle," she said, as she told me good-by.

Yes, I thought, it is a miracle, the simple miracle of prayer. Religion lifted this couple from the low level of selfish bickering to a high plane where the genuine love that existed could become dominant.

Religion works when used in human relationships. If you want happiness in marriage—and of course you do—practice your religion, and if your husband or wife will not join you in prayer and faith, then do all the praying yourself. One person with real faith can bring to bear a spiritual force sufficient to destroy irritating differences. Faith is so potent that one partner alone can lift both to that higher level where understanding and unity are attained.

Religion and love form the foundation of a happy home. They alone can stand the stress and strain of life. Long ago St. Paul wrote a magnificent description of love. Here are some of the things he says about it: "Love suffereth long, and is kind. Love is not easily provoked. Love thinketh no evil. Love beareth all things, believeth all things, hopeth all things, endureth all things." And because love does just those great things is the reason it is necessary as the cornerstone of the home. And love of this quality depends upon religion for its development.

One of the most inspiring of all human experiences is the way real love fights to victory shoulder to shoulder. I have two friends, a young husband and wife who suffered financial reverses. When visiting them one evening recently, I noticed that the wife wanted to say something to me, and when her husband was out of the room for a moment she said: "We're having an awfully hard time of it and John gets so discouraged. He isn't that way by nature, and I hope if you get a chance you'll cheer him up a bit." And then she added with a smile and something in her eye that glistened like a tear, "John's a wonderful fellow, you know."

Later in the evening I happened to be alone with the husband and he said: "Things have been pretty tough lately and sometimes I'm afraid Mary gets a little depressed. If you have a chance before you leave, perk her up a bit." Then, with a voice that was just a shade husky he said, "She's a great girl."

I went away from that home greatly stirred, for I had seen a beautiful thing. I had seen the inspiring sight of two splendid souls, an honest man and a good woman, with love in their hearts, fighting shoulder to shoulder against odds. Will they win? Of course they will! Could that home be broken down? Not in a hundred years. What noble memories the children growing up in it will take on into life! What strong, courageous, clear-minded men and women they will become with a home atmosphere like that.

I believe that many distressing problems in the marriage years and, indeed, throughout all life would be prevented at the source if parents realized the importance of religious faith in the lives of their children. Parents actually contribute to the future unhappiness of their children by failing to give them the benefit of a spiritual background.

The best thing a parent can do for a child is to take him to church, not send him—take him, not intermittently but regularly every Sunday and let him saturate his unconscious mind with the great ideals of religion. Let him hear these truths from the pulpit until they become part of his life, the noblest passages from the Bible. Let him learn to love the great hymns of the Church, which sing of faith and goodness and strength of character. Let him hear sermons: sometimes they may indeed be dull and musty, and frequently they may be over his head, but they will give him the idea that honor, righteousness, and decency are virtues to be cultivated. He will get the conviction so deeply rooted in his mind that it will never be eradicated, that a real man is one of character and honor.

It has to be admitted that not every child so reared in the church has turned out well. But it must also be conceded that the great majority of those children who do turn out well and who live wholesome mental lives, victorious over obsessions and abnormalities of personality, are those who did have a religious upbringing. Give your child a chance for a strong wholesome life; give him a rock foundation to build on, not shifting sand which will wreck his house when the storms come. Do not deprive him of the benefits of religion.

If the child develops character with high ideals, he will conceive of love and marriage as being very beautiful, as a sacrament. He will realize that marriage is an enriching experience in the growth of the soul. He will bring to it, as to an altar, the great virtues which religious faith has implanted in him; the virtues of fidelity, honor, courtesy, kindliness, self-sacrifice, all of which are foundation-stones of happy marriage.

Great-souled men and women can live together in love and peace. Small-souled people bicker and fight and cheat and are thus drawn apart. Real religion creates big-souled people. In the last analysis, then, faith is the answer to successful marriage.

The sublimation of the sex instinct in young people

who are compelled to postpone marriage is a problem. Doctor Blanton as a psychiatrist, and I as a pastor, feel an obligation to present a sensible and workable solution which may be of practical help to young people who seriously want help. This urge, like all human reactions, is subject to the control of the mind. This desire is either intensified or sublimated, depending upon whether the mind dwells on gratification, or holds the urge in check and turns that energy to other outlets. The control and direction of our thoughts is the heart of this problem. When the mind is firmly controlled, the physical instinct cannot dominate. The solution is to fill the mind with interests capable of dominating our thoughts and vital enough to consume our energies. The solution of this problem has been made overcomplicated, whereas actually it is as simple as this: get the mind off the sex instinct and turn it to those intellectual and spiritual values which, when cultivated, are found to be quite as compelling as the instincts relating to the physical organism.

It is rarely possible to drive an idea from the mind merely by determining to do so, regardless of the strength of will which may be employed. Such a direct frontal attack is rarely successful. It actually fixes the thought more firmly on the idea to be expelled due to the emphasis laid upon it. The effective attack is an oblique one, displacing the sex urge by filling the mind with other engrossing interests. This cannot be done by mental effort alone, for thoughts are vagrant and not easily subjected to discipline and orderly control. One must energetically utilize physical, emotional and mental energy in some activity of a worthwhile nature. To the person under strong temptation, this method may seem innocuous, but a sincere and persistent effort of this sort is sufficient. It does capture the interest and correspondingly abates temptation.

There are many activities which offer splendid opportunities for intense interest and enjoyment.

In churches today this need is recognized and emphasis is laid upon youth participation in the church program. I have directed many young men and women who were distressed by this particular problem into organized young people's activity in the church, and have had the pleasure of seeing them acquire the technique of sublimation. This has actually saved—for careers of happiness and usefulness—many young people who otherwise would have wrecked themselves and carried others down with them. They were very attractive and "modern" young people who, despite all their surface sophistication, were desperately fighting a losing battle with an assertive and peremptory antagonist.

When I would suggest attendance at the young people's church gatherings, I could see they were incredulous and sometimes frankly amused. This seemed quite insipid compared to the night clubs and other rendezvous where they were accustomed to spend their leisure time, and struck them as being dull, stodgy, and sanctimonious. I reminded them that their own program of activity was not overly successful; otherwise they would not be consulting me. I pointed out that the church organizations were filled with virile, attractive people, that the programs were creative and modern, and added, "Why come to me unless you have some confidence in my advice?"

I have seen them turn reluctantly to these organizations with ill-concealed doubt and even distaste, but in the great majority of cases they have been happily surprised to find these groups intensely interesting, offering splendid personal contacts, ideas, and ideals that captivated them. They soon found that the old life was the dull and stuffy one by comparison.

I was with a group at a social gathering in the church one night and was struck by the happiness I saw in every face. It was more than just pleasure. It was the outer glow of a deep inward joy. I noted that many faces seemed literally to shine, as is often said of certain characters in the New Testament. One boy, about twenty, with whom I had several times discussed the problems of sex and liquor, took me aside and made this breezy comment: "I want to thank you for getting me into this thing. The old crowd I used to run with seem like a lot of saps to me now. I never really had any fun until I took up with this gang." As I looked at him, eager and convincing, and into eyes that were no longer troubled, I felt the contagion of his joyous spirit. A skillful process of sublimation had changed him, releasing him and developing the higher centers of his personality. The boy's better self had been released by a combination of worthwhile activity, wholesome personal contacts, and his new and active religious faith.

His new-found faith raised his spiritual power to a point where it constituted a virtual immunity to temptation. Power to regulate and control a temptation is a direct result of spiritual conversion. But this is not all. Conversion goes further and modifies our likes and dislikes, so that what once we liked, what appealed to us, has no further attraction. Material or sensuous things, so-called pleasures and dissipations so seemingly important to the pagan-minded person, become undesirable and even boring, or are seen as the evils they are. One wonders why he ever thought them so important; why they ever tempted him.

The man who experiences this upthrust of faith's power does not have to struggle to "be good." It is no sacrifice to him to avoid wrongdoing because wrongdoing is distasteful to him. When one begins to have a hankering for that which is wrong, it simply means that in him spiritual power is declining like the mercury in a thermometer on a cold day. A hunter in the jungle keeps beasts at bay by keeping his campfire blazing. If the fire dies down, the beasts creep in. When the spiritual power flames up, temptation ceases to be a problem. It retreats defeated before the radiance of the new life.

NINE:
The Faith That Heals

The Faith That Heals

Smiley Blanton

THE POWERFUL INFLUENCE OF UNHAPPY EMOTIONS ON the mind and body was long overlooked by physicians. Only in comparatively recent years has it been taken into fullest consideration.

This oversight was due to the materialistic philosophy which dominated science during the eighteenth and nineteenth centuries, a philosophy which thought of man as a sort of chemical machine. To be sure, in this materialistic phase science did discover the control of such diseases as typhoid fever, smallpox, and diphtheria, but it failed to provide the physician with the secret of nervous and mental disturbances which often seriously affect the function of the various bodily organs. It failed to do anything for the great number of nervous and mental breakdowns which constantly swell the hospital lists.

This unfortunate materialistic conception viewed man's mind and body as separate things. One physician, some forty years ago, even wrote that, if he could cut his patients' heads off when they were sick, he could get them well much quicker. It did not occur to him that it might be better to treat the heads. If a person is ill his head must not only be left on, but perhaps even treated first.

The modern physician does not look upon man's mental, moral, and emotional life as separated from his physical life: he thinks of man as a unit, a mental-physical unit.

When this more rational concept began to prevail, and the physician began to be aware of the patient as an indivisible unit, compact of mind and body, has healing art made almost miraculous advances. Illness, he learned, was not caused solely by abnormalities of the chemistry of the body or by weakening of the body's defenses against germs. It could also be caused by emotional maladjustments which give rise to morbid fears and hatreds and in that way cause actual changes in the body's chemistry. Indigestion, abnormal functioning of the heart, high blood pressure, asthma, various pains, and chronic fatigue, as well as nervous and mental breakdowns, may be due primarily to emotional and spiritual maladjustments—the inability to feel secure, to love, to find one's proper place in the world's scheme, to have faith.

The importance of courage and faith in the fight to get well becomes evident. Physicians have often observed that of two patients with an apparently equal chance to survive, one lives and the other dies. Every surgeon knows how much more dangerous it is to operate on a frightened patient than on a confident, fearless one. The decisive factor seems to be the presence or absence of the will to live—a will to live backed by a strong, sometimes even unconscious, courage and faith.

Even in the entirely physical illness the sick person's mental reaction is almost as important in evaluating his chance of recovery as is his physical reaction. In such obviously physical conditions as pneumonia, or tuberculosis, or diseases of the heart valves, or even, let us say, a broken leg, there is not only a physical problem but an important attendant emotional problem as well. It is the way a person feels about his illness which determines to a large extent whether or not he is going to get well at all. Certainly it determines how he is going to live with his illness if it does continue; it determines both the length and the nature of his convalescence.

There is a touching and also amusing story told of the very early Kentucky frontier. It was after the year of 1782, during which about one-fifth of a pathetically small community had been killed by the Indians. There were never enough hands to do even the simplest job. Each adult was invaluable, and each child a burden.

Mr. Jo Craig, a preacher more famous for his frank approach to problems than for his eloquence or diplomacy, was called to the bedside of a woman to hear her dying words. Mr. Craig looked at her a few seconds and then he said to her, "Hannah, if you die and leave all these helpless little children for some other woman to care for with things as they are now, it will be the meanest thing you ever did in your life!" It is said that it made Hannah so angry that she sat up in bed "fever and all and read him out of the church." She got well and survived to rear her family and do her share of the work. In his frankness he had restored her courage and her will to live.

But not all cases are so simple. Mr. W. J.'s was a case of fracture of the thigh. He was under the care of an excellent surgeon, and the bones knitted perfectly. Normally he should have been completely well in six months. But although he was a man of only forty-two when he had the fracture, he was practically a semi-invalid for five or six years. He worried incessantly about the slight limp in his walk and talked incessantly about each slight twinge. He was even afraid that the bone might "come unknitted," although he was shown the improbability of this.

Finally it was brought out, in psychiatric interviews, that he was driving his car when the accident occurred and that the man in the other car was killed. Although he was exonerated by the court, he always had the feeling that with more care and more alertness he could himself have avoided the accident. He had developed an unconscious sense of guilt over the death of the other man, and was punishing himself for it.

The invalidism had also served to hold what he had thought to be the waning affection of his wife, which was, in the first place, what had made him reckless. It was possible to make him see that he was not meeting his problem on an adult basis and to help him to a greater adequacy. It was also possible for the minister to help him get a feeling of relief from the sense of guilt, and to restore his confidence in his right to get well.

Heart disorders are another type of case in which the attitude of the patient toward his physical difficulty is most important.

Mr. R., a well-known business man of 61, had an attack of coronary thrombosis. In most cases of this sort, if the patient is willing to adjust his life, he can live for many successful years. But Mr. R. had a driving necessity for business that never permitted him to take any thought for himself or for his family. He justified himself by feeling that he was taking care of the family's future in advance. His family respected and loved him, but they were never very close to him because they never had the chance to be. As he grew older he became more irritable. The slightest opposition would arouse his anger and bring his blood pressure up.

After his attack no one was able to persuade him to readjust his life. He grew more and more irritable, easily flew into rages at the hospital routine, and finally left before he was dismissed. He went back to work and very shortly had another attack. He retired from his work and retreated into his home, where he devoted his time and attention to worrying about each small symptom.

He was a pitiful figure whom no one could help because he had no faith in anyone. He managed to keep alive for ten years longer, but it could hardly be called living.

On the other hand, Mr. S., who was an easy-going, cheerful man, found himself at the age of 63 a semi-invalid with a heart lesion. His doctor wisely encouraged him to feel that his more useful days were still ahead of him, and that he could still be of service in the world, even though he must change his routine completely.

Mr. S. took it as a challenge to his ingenuity, rather than a sentence. He came eventually to the church clinic and asked us to help him work out a program that would keep him active mentally and happy, but allow him the minimum amount of physical effort.

A small amount of time each day was set aside for him to attend to necessary business affairs. The rest of his interest was easily diverted into a certain hospital board on which he had always worked and with which he was now free to go further. His advice was very valuable to them and hours that he spent in bed were often devoted to working out the various problems that they presented to him.

His new routine also gave him an opportunity to see more of his wife and children, and when he died at the age of 84, his family had the feeling that his last twenty years, spent under what to some people would have been intolerable conditions, were, instead, the happiest of his life.

In certain disorders contentment, or at the very least passive acceptance of conditions, is so essential that the patient has little chance to survive without it.

Mr. T. was seen in a hospital in the South. He came in suffering from pulmonary tuberculosis. But after some weeks in the hospital, when he should have been showing some improvement, he was actually worse. When he talked it was with a low, depressed voice, and it shortly became obvious that he had little desire to live. When the psychiatrist talked to him the following things were brought out.

He had had a good position, but his eyes had failed him and he had lost it. His family had used up all its resources and were in desperate circumstances. Then he confided that he had a small paid-up insurance policy, and that if he died his family would have at least enough to tide them over the coming winter, and possibly to make a new start in life.

Mr. T. had an uncle with whom he had never been on very good terms and to whom he had refused to turn for help. But the minister of the uncle's church was gotten in touch with, and then it turned out that the uncle's little store was booming on account of a large hospital that had been built near it, and that he would actually be grateful for the help of his nephew's wife and the two oldest children, and would be glad to help them establish a small home.

Mr. T.'s attitude and condition changed entirely. He became cheerful and confident and saw the possibility of work for himself also when he should recover. He was able to leave the hospital in six months and four years later he was still living and well. This was a case in which social service had given the man a chance to make a recovery. Without a change in his attitude he would in all probability have been dead.

There are cases in which minor illnesses seem actually to have been blessings in disguise, because they brought to a head the needs and the difficulties of an individual or a family. The case of Mr. J., who had the thigh injury, was such. The heart lesion of Mr. S. was not an unmixed calamity. And certainly the tuberculosis of Mr. T was in the end an advantage to himself and to his family.

There are times in people's lives when an illness or an operation focuses attention on them and brings to the forefront conditions that were very destructive to the person and that would otherwise have been ignored.

Such was the case of Mrs. C. J. Her husband had become more and more immersed in business and committees of one sort or another, so that his evenings, as well as his days, were spent away from home. Her two daughters and her son had married and moved to homes of their own. In her very busy life there had been no time for hobbies or outside activities, or, she thought, even for church.

Eventually, left so much to herself, she began to be depressed and overly introspective. Eventually her physician recommended a slight operation to correct a very minor matter.

Her absence from theh house, and her presence in the hospital, served to arouse her children and her husband to her value to them and to her needs as a human being. Her two daughters took rooms at a nearby hotel to be on call. Her husband dropped some of his involved activities in order to plan a trip with her when she should be well again. Neighbors called to express their affection. The minister called and asked her to come back into active church work.

The operation was merely a minor event in this revelatory series. She returned home to a new atmosphere, new outside interests in her neighborhood and her church, and to a new realization of her own place in the hearts of her family.

Not all illnesses end so happily as some of these: not all tragedies resolve themselves nor are all burdens lifted. But truly all burdens are lightened by courage, and unhappiness is relieved of its load of infantile guilt by understanding and insight. Pity and love for the other members of our race who struggle along an uneven and discouraged road must not obscure the necessity for love and forgiveness of oneself.

The capacity for faith springs from the capacity for love; and faith, which has been defined for all time as the "substance of things hoped for, the evidence of things not seen," must be a vigorous and growing emotion if our spirits are to survive.

The Faith That Heals

NORMAN VINCENT PEALE

TRAVELING IN THE PROVINCE OF ALBERTA in Western Canada, I was shown a natural phenomenon known locally as "the mingling of the waters." Here two important rivers, the Kicking Horse and the Yoho, merge, and, under the name of the former, flow on through a manifold series of canyons and valleys in settings of superb scenic wonder. At the point of meeting, the Yoho has a dull chalk color derived from a glacier which feeds it glacial sediment of the same hue.

The Kicking Horse River also rises from a melting glacier and at its source has the same content and color as the Yoho, but runs through two mountain lakes before meeting the latter. It flows first into Lake O'Hara, which checks its swift pace so that its glacial sediment, held in suspension by the current, may sink into the calm waters of the lake. It resumes its rapid flow and presently enters Lake Waptka, a still broader and deeper body of water. Its headlong rush is again quieted by still waters, and the silt not deposited in the first lake is precipitated into the second. The two lakes are a natural filtering system which sends the river on its way a clear, sparkling mountain stream, so that when it meets the silt-laden Yoho, it cuts a path of blue across that river's chalky waters.

In the same way faith calms and cleanses the lives of modern men and women. Their lives have been discolored and burdened by an accumulation of harmful foreign thoughts. They have consciously or otherwise accepted much extraneous matter in the shape of wrong attitudes, stresses, emotional disturbances, and guilt, so much so that they have formed a basis of ill health. Some men and women have been fortunate in discovering the secret of eliminating these causes of emotional and physical distress. As the river is cleansed of its sediment by flowing into a deep, quiet lake, so they turn their minds to the deep places of religion. Peace comes to them, and, what is more important, those fears and sins which have clogged the mind and disorganized the emotions are cast off. Perhaps this is what the writer of the Twenty-Third Psalm means when he says, "He leadeth me beside the still waters; he restoreth my soul."

Many people today *could* have good health, free from emotional ills and from much sickness of all types, if they would practice faith and invite its healing power.

On a recent Sunday I was standing before the pulpit, as is my custom after a church service, greeting those who wished to speak with me. I noticed a young man, very agitated and obviously under great nervous strain, waiting impatiently. He said, "I must see you alone at once." I replied that due to the pressure of my Sunday schedule I could not see him until Monday in the regular interview period, but he persisted and seemed so beside himself that I sent him to the interview room, saying I would see him there presently.

I opened the conversation by asking him where he lived, and he said Boston. But the accent sounded like north of Boston to me, and when I smilingly said so, he explained that he originally came from the lake and woods region of Maine. It happened to be a very warm

Sunday and I remarked how pleasant it would be if we were at that moment in the north woods beside a quiet lake. I said, "How cool it would be and how restful, what a pleasure to get a whiff of that pine-laden air into our lungs."

This seemed an opening and I talked on at some length about the quiet woods, the still lake, the distant mountains, the peace and strength of that glorious region from which he came as a boy. I remarked that it did me good merely to reflect on such a quiet scene, where God's peace was to found. It was only a step from a talk about the Maine woods to a talk about God and His peace. I told him of a fact which has helped me, that by simply opening a gate in our minds we can walk with that great, calm Soul who long ago said, "Come unto me, . . . and I will give you rest." In the mind we can hear His voice saying, "Peace, be still." The peace of lake and woods is transitory, but He said: "My Peace I give unto you: not as the world giveth, give I unto you. Let not your heart be troubled."

As I talked, I noticed that he grew more composed, and asked him to join me in prayer. He nodded, and I prayed that God's peace would come into his heart and fill him with a great, deep and abiding calm. When I had finished, he immediately began a prayer of his own, but to my surprise he did not plead for anything, he did not implore God to give him peace, as a desperate man would. Instead, he reverently said, "I thank you, Lord, for making me so quiet inside." It was an excellent phrase, "quiet inside." He told me later he had slept badly for weeks and that he had been greatly troubled by headaches and digestive disorders.

I then asked, "Now, what was the problem you wanted

to talk to me about?" He held out his hand to me and said: "I think now I can solve it myself. I feel I am able to handle it now." What had happened? He had turned to God, and God had touched his disturbed mind with a healing peace. As a result, it was swept clean and its power to think reorganized. His tense anxiety was relieved and he became conscious of a new access of power, and a delight in the feel of this new-found strength.

One might conceivably fall back from this level of peace into the old shadowy fear-haunted ways, for the habit grooves are there. But such an experience may, on the other hand, be so completely curative that one is permanently healed. The important fact in this healing by faith was, of course, that the young man did not stop to consider doubts, but sharply projected his trust through these doubts straight to God, and thus instantly the spiritual power was released, and flowed into his mind with the above result.

An eminent psychiatrist recently said, "Prayer is the greatest power in this world, and it is a pity we do not make use of it." This man of science, whose field is mental healing and the development of the personality, declared that when he can get his patients to practice the simple art of prayer, he has them well on the road to recovery. Well-informed and thoughtful modern people are beginning to recognize that not only peace of mind, out enhanced effectiveness in work and daily living are direct results of this practice, which we have been accustomed to associate only with the pious. It is very significant that the scientific study of man has resulted in a pronounced emphasis upon the ancient art of prayer, which some people thought was outmoded. The old-fashioned man nowadays is the man who does not pra'

Prayer is in style again, and for the very good reason that we have learned we cannot get along without it if we want to be normal and efficient.

Some men have their minds so open to the Infinite Power that they have a remarkably close connection with God. The governor of a mid-western state is reported to have said that his method for solving industrial strikes is to pray and to advise the representatives of labor and capital to do the same. Many people have laughed heartily at this apparently naive idea, but it is a fact that this governor usually succeeds in settling the strikes, whereas human wisdom without benefit of prayer has not always been so successful. The governor says he believes it is possible to "run a pipe-line" to God. The illustration is not all that is to be desired, but it is true that when men turn to God with simple faith, the abundance with which He pours out His might indeed require a "pipe-line." Here lies the explanation, in part at least, of the growing respect for, and the use of, the old art of prayer.

Prayer, which is a manifestation of faith, works miracles. What is meant by prayer? Certainly, not the idle recitation of mumbling of formulas, or even a beseeching of God. Prayer, as Dr. Alexis Carrel, the renowned scientist, describes it, is the surrender of the personality to God, as the blank canvas stands before the painter and in effect says, I am empty, fill me as you will. So prayer is man standing before God, his whole life open for God's will to be done through him.

Once the disciples were watching Jesus at prayer. They were fascinated by what they saw. The expression of his untenance changed. A strong inner light illumined it. weariness dropped away as by magic. His tones d with a deep and vibrant strength and his entire demeanor was exalted and confident. Before their very eyes he was drawing upon hidden sources of energy and joy. "Lord," they cried excitedly, "Lord, teach us to pray." They had seen real prayer in actual demonstration. This is the kind of prayer that unlocked power in an astonishing way.

What do we mean by a miracle? A miracle is a phenomenon not explainable by existing natural laws; it is a supernatural law. It is something which, according to usual procedure, does not happen. It is the attainment of results beyond human power. The idea of a miracle has often been associated with the bizarre or grotesque, which made it difficult to believe. We mean something different by a miracle. It is the operation of the supernatural, or God's power through the receptive believing of man accomplishing that which human strength and wisdom are unable to achieve. We naturally do not believe in any grotesque procedure, but we firmly have the opinion that we need a new faith in the power of God to work wonders in our lives today as in the past.

Long ago the disciples saw Christ working wonders, and when they marveled at it he said, "Greater things than these shall ye do." And they did them. But we are not doing these greater things. Why? The answer is we do not have the faith they had. We do not believe as sincerely and so we lack the "miraculous" power offered us.

Prayer really works miracles when our faith is active. The New Testament tells us: "The effectual fervent prayer of a righteous man availeth much." Many miracles of prayer and faith are taking place today in the field of physical and mental health.

This was once a very important aspect of Christianity. The New Testament is full of accounts of healing by

Christ and his disciples. The tendency of the Christian religion has been to ignore its healing element. But now that science is acknowledged, and its real harmony with religion better established, it is becoming evident that even as science has set free forces in the material world, so a more scientific application of prayer and faith tends to set free once more the healing forces which are described in the New Testament as being of usual occurrence. There is now, I feel, a happy tendency for psychiatry, general medicine, and surgery to work together with religion, each in its own realm, to be sure, but with sympathy and understanding in the common cause of healing body, mind, and soul.

One doctor put it very well: "I treated my patient, and God healed him." If we will avail ourselves of the best that medical science can give us and at the same time by faith and prayer put ourselves in the hands of God, being sure to pray always that God's will be done whatever that may involve, we shall receive curative and restorative forces of remarkable efficacy. The head of the medical service is a great university hospital said, "One should send for his minister as he sends for his doctor when he becomes ill." That is to say, God helps the sick in two ways, through the science of medicine and surgery, and through the science of faith and prayer. This latter brings the mind and spirit of the sick into harmony with God. The physician receives The Superlative cooperation, and healing establishes itself.

My brother, Dr. Robert C. Peale, a physician and surgeon, says, "Because of the abiding faith and trust the injured or sick person has in Almighty God, as a surgeon I constantly see recoveries that were thought impossible. I also see poor results because of an attempted cure by religion or science alone. I am therefore convinced that there is a definite and fixed relationship between religion and science, and that God has given us both as weapons against disease and unhappiness, but administered together for the benefit of mankind, their possibilities are unlimited."

In a certain city not long ago a man came up to speak with me after I had completed an address and told me he had had a nervous breakdown and despite every care and effort, made no improvement. He had then happened to read something I said to the effect that "the power of faith and prayer helps to heal sickness." He said, "I was up against it and so was willing to try anything." With a new and desperate interest he had turned to the New Testament and greedily read the promises it contains, such as, "According to your faith be it unto you." Finally, one day, he had said to himself, "I believe there's really something to this." By prayer and faith he gave himself into God's hands, with the result that when he saw me that night he could report that he was a new man physically, mentally, and spiritually.

Later I investigated his case and found that he was in every sense a rational, sensible, upstanding citizen of his community—in every way a competent witness to the value of religion in dealing with sickness. As he left me he said, "It's a great combination—prayer and my doctor."

Simple faith in God opens our lives in an amazing manner to the forces of healing and strength and growth. All serious students of mankind know that man's essential quality is not physical or material but spiritual. A man can live a purely physical and material life for a while, but he will be beaten eventually because he has cut himself off from the source of life-giving vitality. Like a pool of water separated from the living waters of a running stream, he presently becomes stagnant and unhealthy. He becomes unhappy and ineffectual because he is cut off from the flow of this life-giving force. Simple faith and surrender to God correct this condition. It is remarkable what a sincere attempt to attune ourselves with God's power will do for us physically, mentally, and spiritually.

The distinguished social worker, Muriel Lester, tells us she could no longer stand the strain of her activities, and consequently had a nervous collapse. An unutterable depression filled her mind and for weeks she suffered from physical and mental weakness. One day she read that if a straw is laid in the great Gulf Stream in line with its currents, the essential quality of the Gulf Stream water will flow through the straw. It occurred to her to wonder whether if a human life should put itself willingly in the direction of the flow of God's spiritual power, whether that power would not in essence pass with healing strength through that life. She determined to try it. By the practice of simple faith she completely surrendered her life to God. She placed herself, body, mind, and spirit, in the direction of the flow of God's power. Not all at once, but presently, like dawn stealing across the darkened world, the quiet strength of God came into her life, endowing her with vitality and an amazing capacity for outstanding constructive work. Our generation is just beginning to awaken to the tremendous possibilities inherent in religious faith, which greatly enhances the efficiency of all human endeavor.

In view of these and other impressive truths about healing through faith, and the fact that these truths are so little known, it is not surprising that the professor in a university class in mental hygiene made the announcement that he would not disclose the name of the textbook used in preparing his lectures to his class until the end of the semester. When that time arrived, he announced that the textbook was the New Testament, and declared it "the most thoroughgoing and competent work in the field." He advised his students to practice the principles of the New Testament, that it was not only the best guide for morals but also an aid to good health.

In this volume I have stressed the fact that the great secret of life is to surrender oneself to God's will by an act of faith. I cannot close without once again declaring most positively that we can solve any problem of personality if we completely turn to God and open our minds and hearts to His will. To do so inevitably makes available healing and curative forces beyond anything yet discovered in this world. The New Testament, our Supreme book on psychiatry and religion, the noblest volume about life ever written, unequivocally declares that faith is the golden key which releases a power so astounding that we cannot begin to appreciate it.

If we will only believe, there is no limit to the blessings God will shower upon us. We are told that Christ came to give us "the abundant life." That is something far beyond the narrow, limited, frustrated lives most of us live. The whole emphasis of the New Testament, which we so tragically miss, is that God wants to pour out His blessings until "your cup runneth over." No blessing is too great, no power too strong, no victory too complete. All is yours for the *asking*.

There is a strange statement in the New Testament. Christ had been depicting the wonders God wants to give to people and was telling them what they could have and do and be. But He saw they did not believe Him, would not accept what He offered, and we read that, "He marveled because of their unbelief." He was bewildered because those who were offered *everything* chose to continue living on *nothing*. So today the average man lives on spiritual relief when all of God's riches are his for the *taking*.

Let one final story from the New Testament explain what can happen to any man at any moment when he truly believes.

Peter and John were on their way into the Temple when they saw a lame beggar sitting by the beautiful Temple gate. He had been lame from birth. Long years of helplessness had also crippled him in spirit. Hopelessness and a sense of futility had eaten into his soul. He could see no hope, no future. Wheedling a stray coin from a compassionate passer-by now and then was all he could expect from life.

He could not know what this day was to mean to him, how his life was to be changed. Slumped wearily on the Temple step, his eyes dully staring at the ground, a grimy hand outstretched for alms, he was suddenly aware that two men stood before him.

Peter and John stopped. They too had once been frustrated men, albeit in a different way. They knew that money was no solution to this man's problem. Given a fortune, he would still be the same weak mortal. His difficulty, they realized, was an inner malady, not an outer condition. They recalled that their discerning Master had once told a man that he "must be born again." The Great Physician had indicated an inward cure, a complete change, in effect the equivalent of rebirth. The man must become a new man. This superior wisdom marked Jesus Christ as possessing insight beyond all others who have to do with people. Christianity has always stressed conversion. It does not do things by halves; is not content with partial cures. It holds that the only effective method is to attack the disease at the core and cut it out at the roots.

So Peter saw that this crippled beggar needed faith both in God and in himself. Give him that, and the rest would take care of itself—"Seek ye first the Kingdom of God, . . . and all these things shall be added unto you." Here the story takes a very significant turn. Peter, fixing his eyes on the man, who kept on staring hopelessly at the ground, said, "Look on us." He wanted by magnetism to draw the man's mind away from himself and his misery. He wanted the man to look up and to see two men who like himself had been weak and defeated but were made strong by the amazing genius of Christ.

"Look on us," demanded Peter again, as his direct gaze seemed to bore into the dull brain before him. It was difficult for the man to look up, as he had looked down for so long. It is always difficult for men to leave their chains which, hated at first, become almost comfortably familiar after long imprisonment. "Look on us!"—the words, the tone, the suggestion of power beat into the man's mind. Slowly his eyes came up, irresistibly drawn until they were on a level with Peter's. They saw a weather-beaten face, a face strong and seamed like a granite cliff, but a cliff which reflected the sun. But it was Peter's eyes that caught and held his. His eyes were kindly but keen and steady too, and seemed to say, "You have something great in you. You can, you can."

Continuing to hold the lame man's gaze, Peter said, "In the name of Jesus Christ of Nazareth rise up and walk." Whereupon the beggar's eyes opened wide in fright and disbelief. They flinched under Peter's determined look and command, and seemed to complain, "I cannot, I've been lame since birth; what you ask is impossible." But Peter's eyes, filled with indomitable faith, held him fast. "In the name of Jesus Christ of Nazareth rise up and walk."

Stiffly, but as if drawn irresistibly by a magnet, the man, still looking into Peter's compelling eyes, put out his hand and slowly rose to his feet. Gingerly he tested the ankle bones that had never exercised their function. Slowly and with growing confidence he rested his full weight on them. A look of joyous incredulity spread over his face. Hope like a light flashed up in his dull eyes. An involuntary cry of happiness, the joyous cry of a man suddenly delivered from a living death, issued from his lips. He sensed his new power and forgot his weakness. Little wonder, then, as the Scripture says, that he leaped and ran and praised God and proceeded to the Temple with Peter and John to give thanks to Almighty God for his deliverance.

This story is told in the most worthy and reliable book ever written. Immerse yourself in that book, believe in it with a whole heart, practice its principles, especially its technique of applying faith; and I assure you that you will make the great discovery that for your every problem, FAITH IS THE ANSWER.